THE EXPERTS' GUIDE
TO THE
BABY YEARS

The Experts' Guide to the Baby Years

100 Things Every Parent Should Know

CREATED BY

SAMANTHA ETTUS

CLARKSON POTTER/PUBLISHERS
NEW YORK

This title may be purchased for business or promotional use or for special sales. For information, please write to Special Markets Department, Random House, Inc., 1745 Broadway, MD 6-3, New York, NY 10019, or e-mail specialmarkets@randomhouse.com.

Published in the United States by Clarkson Potter/Publishers, an imprint of the Crown Publishing Group, a division of Random House, Inc., New York.

www.crownpublishing.com
www.clarksonpotter.com

Clarkson N. Potter is a trademark and Potter and colophon are registered trademarks of Random House, Inc.

Library of Congress Cataloging-in-Publication Data is available upon request.

ISBN-13: 978-0-307-34208-9
ISBN-10: 0-307-34208-5

Printed in the United States of America

Design by Jennifer K. Beal

10 9 8 7 6 5 4 3 2 1

First Edition

CONTENTS

CONTENTS

CONTENTS

CONTENTS

CONTENTS

CONTENTS

ACKNOWLEDGMENTS

This book—with all of its moving parts—would not have been possible without the wisdom and passion of the 100 expert contributors. I am so grateful to them for their contributions to this book and to their fields, and for inadvertently enriching my own life as a new mom.

My deepest appreciation goes to my love, Mitch Jacobs, my husband, best friend, and favorite person. Our newest adventure is our most challenging yet rewarding and I couldn't dream of a better partner for it. Our beautiful daughter, Ella, is so lucky to have you as her dad. I wake up every day (and as a new mom, many times during the night) with a smile on my face because of you and our delicious baby.

I also want to extend my thanks to Jennifer Joel, who excels at everything she takes on. She is the ideal brainstorming partner, devoted friend, and agent. And to Katie Karoussos, David Baum, Juda Kallus, Dan Fannon, and Josh Lipschutz and all of the members of my professional team who have shown me such loyalty and support during this chapter of my career. To my editor, Aliza Fogelson, whose talent and hard work transformed this book from great to invaluable. And to Amy Corley, Tina Constable, Philip Patrick, Doris Cooper, and, of course, Lauren Shakely and the entire Clarkson Potter team for their support of The Experts' Guides. Thanks also go to our own team of baby experts . . . Dr. Barbara Landreth, Ella's brilliant, kind, and overall exceptional pediatrician, and Dr. Sherine Russell, Joanne Jones, and Lourdes Chung.

And finally, thank you to the friends and family who continue to provide me with inspiring ideas, love, and support on my professional and personal journeys.

With gratitude,
Sam

INTRODUCTION

I don't think it was possible to prepare for childbirth more than my husband and I did. We were determined to do it naturally so we signed up for both Lamaze and the Bradley Method (why settle for one!) and we pored over a multitude of books. By my due date, I had taken enough classes to qualify as a birthing coach, but because of our breach baby my epidural-intent friends ended up with deliveries far more natural than my planned C-section.

The magic of Ella Madeline's arrival erased the memory of any pain I had endured during pregnancy. And while I lay in a joyous fog with all six pounds ten ounces of Ella sleeping on my chest, I became amused by how prepared we had been for the delivery yet how unprepared we were for what happened next.

Like all new parents, we were inundated almost immediately with a stew of conflicting advice. Both unsolicited and welcome opinions flew at us like spitballs, and the dos and don'ts were even more numerous than the sources. Don't spoil the baby. Do offer endless affection. Don't worry about her poop. Do call your doctor if she hasn't pooped. Don't let her cry. Do use a pacifier. The barrage of advice wove a tapestry of ongoing worries and doubts in me. And my concerns were not confined to the baby. How would my husband and I make time for romance? Would my in-laws help out with the baby? I craved a reliable and unbiased source of information. As when forging ahead to any destination, it would help to know where I was going before I arrived

This led to my quest for wisdom we *could* count on: expert advice. I put this book together as I was preparing to give birth and I finished it in the months after. I polled countless new moms to find out what they wished they had known in the first two years and the top 100 topics they raised are included in the pages that follow.

My husband and I were the guinea pigs, devouring the chapters in the hopes of removing some of the mystery from parenting. The book is intended to provide solutions for both your baby's needs and your own. Just like putting on your oxygen mask first, caring for yourself will enable you to take better care of Baby.

From renowned pediatricians to academics and celebrities, the experts in these pages are accomplished and varied. I fell in love with Philip M. Tierno Jr.'s take on germs after watching him show Matt Lauer why an escalator is no place to put his hands. I solicited name expert Laura Wattenberg after her book became my own baby-naming bible. Dr. Harvey Karp's five-S plan for calming a baby made Ella's transition from the womb a seamless one. We relied on Dr. Marc Weissbluth's magic to get her sleeping through the night. And who better than Kate Spade to share tricks on packing a diaper bag or fitness guru Pamela Peeke to tell you how to get back in shape after childbirth?

Like all new parents, I dreamed of staying one step ahead of my baby—of anticipating her teething before I discovered the pool of drool and of planning a date night with my husband before we ended up believing baby talk was our sole language of love. With this in mind, I organized the book in a loosely chronological way (since every baby is on a different timeline!) to give all new parents a fighting chance of remaining at least one chapter ahead of their baby's next need, and their needs, too.

My enchantment with Ella is limitless and as a first-time mother my maternal knowledge gap was just as vast. I have counted on the experts found in the pages of this book to guide me through my first year of motherhood and their wisdom is bound to be an invaluable partner to you as you embark on your own parenting journey.

Best of luck along the way, and please drop me a line to let me know how it's going . . .

—SAMANTHA (AKA ELLA'S MOM)
ELLASMOM@EXPERTSMEDIA.COM

CHOOSE A NAME

LAURA WATTENBERG

Laura Wattenberg is the developer of name analysis software

and the author of The Baby Name Wizard.

"**S**o, have you settled on a name yet?"

As the clock winds down many parents find themselves surprisingly stumped, still searching for the perfect name to express their tastes—and satisfy the whole family. A name choice encompasses fashion and tradition, values and dreams.

Whether you've talked yourself out of your favorite name or debated your partner to a standstill, try these strategies for getting past some common roadblocks:

OUR FAVORITE NAME IS TOO POPULAR

You want a distinctive name for your daughter. *She's* not going to be one of five Jennifers in her class. But now it turns out that Abigail, your cherished favorite, is a top-ten name!

Don't toss aside that beloved name just yet. A popularity rank doesn't tell the whole story. First off, there are no "Jennifers" in this new generation—no names you'll find in every classroom.

Parents are naming more creatively, so even the number-one name today is only a fraction as popular as the hot names of past generations.

A name's impact also depends on the way it blends in with the sound of the times. April was a popular choice in the 1970s and 1980s—more popular than the name Kristin. But Kristin feels more common because it traveled in a pack of similar names (Krista-Kirsten-Kristi-Krystal). A name with a unique sound, like April, can stay fresh despite its popularity. If the name you love does travel with a pack (Jaden-Braeden-Hayden-Kaiden), don't despair. Remember that "popular" simply means well liked, so people are likely to respond well to the name and to your child.

THE TWO OF US CAN'T AGREE

As the birth date looms closer, a name dispute can turn combustible. Ratchet down the hostilities by taking pen to paper. Go to separate rooms and each write down your six top choices. (No, writing Eleanor six times doesn't count.) Then trade papers and each choose the two names you find least objectionable. That's your short list.

Give a game effort to agree on one of the short-list names. If you can't, use it as your reference point for finding a compromise. Break down what exactly appeals to you about each name. If he likes the gentle grace of Olivia and she likes the exotic uniqueness of Xanthia, look for a rare but delicate alternative (Lavinia, Raphaela).

NOTHING GOES WITH OUR LAST NAME

A full name can be like a little line of poetry with rhyme and meter. You may choose a name you love, only to test it out with your surname and find it falls flat. (Middle names are no solution; they'll quickly disappear from your daily usage, leaving the awkward combo to last a lifetime.) If your compositions aren't working, try putting the names aside for a moment and focusing purely on sounds.

Cast about for some common word, no matter how silly, that sounds good with your last name. Try looking around your kitchen and saying the results out loud: "Grinder Anderson?" No thanks. "Banana Anderson?" Hardly. "Licorice Anderson?" Hmm . . . silly, but catchy. Now look for names with a sound pattern similar to Licorice (like Nicholas). At the very least you'll consider some new possibilities—and lighten the mood.

I'M JUST OVERWHELMED

Okay, forget the checklists and popularity charts. Here's a one-step plan to a name you can feel good about: imagine that it's you starting out in life. Knowing everything you know about the world, what name would you want representing *you*? A name you would feel confident bearing is certain to make a fine welcome gift for your child.

BUDGET FOR A NEW BABY

LIZ PULLIAM WESTON

Liz Pulliam Weston is the author of two books, including Your Credit Score: How to Fix, Improve, and Protect the 3-Digit Number That Shapes Your Financial Future. *She is a personal finance columnist for MSN Money and author of the question-and-answer column "Money Talk," which appears in newspapers throughout the country. She was formerly a personal finance writer for the* Los Angeles Times.

The nesting instinct can cause expecting parents to embark on all kinds of expensive preparations. If you're not careful, you can find yourself blowing thousands of dollars on furniture, clothing, equipment, and other purchases before the tot even arrives.

The key to surviving this period with your financial health intact is to have a plan and stick to it. Otherwise, the $4 billion baby products industry and your own oscillating emotions will lure you into overspending.

Here's your plan of attack:

Factor in your fixed costs. Talk to your insurer or hospital about how much of the delivery costs you'll be expected to shoulder. Find out how much it will cost to add your new child to your health insurance. Explore child-care options and costs if you'll be returning to work. Adjust your budget to reflect these expenses. If you decide to stay home, you can determine how your forgone salary will impact your financial situation. You may discover that you aren't missing out on as much income as you thought, once taxes, commuting costs, and child-care expenses are factored in.

Figure out what items you really need—and what you don't. Talk to experienced parents, consult some guidebooks, and use the Internet to compile your must-have list, along with the expected price of each item. Don't assume that if a baby store stocks a product you have to have it; many parents discover the money they spent on a coordinated linen set or a deluxe wipes warmer would have been better invested in a college fund.

Accept donations. Your friends and family may start offering their hand-me-down baby gear as soon as you announce that you're pregnant; take them up on their offers after making sure the stuff meets current safety standards. Go easy on buying clothes and stuffed animals. You'll probably get plenty of both. Your loved ones will likely want to throw you a shower, and you can ask for whatever items haven't already been donated.

Don't disdain yard sales and consignment shops. You'll find a wealth of gently used or even never-used items at a fraction of their retail prices. To sanitize plastic items, use a weak bleach solution or disposable cleaning wipes; clothing and most stuffed toys can be sent through the washing machine.

Consider breastfeeding. The La Leche League estimates the average mother can save $2,000 in her child's first year by breastfeeding. If breastfeeding is not possible, you can reduce formula costs by using coupons, asking your pediatrician for samples, and seeing if you qualify for insurance coverage if your child requires a specialized formula because of allergies.

Diaper defensively. The average child will go through more than 5,000 diapers before potty training is complete, according to Ohio State University estimates. You can save hundreds of dollars by buying generic diapers, using coupons, and taking advantage of sales. Using cloth diapers can also save you money, although some of the savings will be offset by increased laundering costs.

Shop judiciously to fill in the gaps. Bring your list with you on any shopping trips and consider doing research in advance to make sure you're getting the best prices. Don't get ahead of yourself; buy only the items you're sure you'll use in the first few months after your baby arrives. The tricycle, the videos, and the basketball hoop can wait.

Pay cash. Don't get in the habit of using credit cards to absorb the extra expenses of a baby or you may find yourself on the road to bankruptcy. Paying cash can provide you with the discipline to stay within your budget and avoid disastrous splurges.

Keep receipts. Maintain a separate folder just for baby-related receipts. You will likely end up raiding it to return unused items.

How about ongoing costs after the child is born? Those will depend on numerous factors, including your lifestyle and the type and amount of child care you might need. Most people should expect their living expenses to rise about 10 percent with every child added to the family. With careful planning you can keep those extra costs from busting your budget.

DESIGN A NURSERY

WENDY BELLISSIMO

Wendy Bellissimo is president and chief designer for Wendy

Bellissimo Media, Inc., and the author of Nesting: Lifestyle

Inspirations for Your Growing Family. *A favorite among*

celebrities, Bellissimo has designed nurseries for Kelly Ripa,

Brooke Shields, and Denise Richards.

The ultimate baby room embodies a calming yet inspiring environment. Function and practicality are just as important as the look you are trying to create. Choose items that will grow with your child or that you will be able to use for your next baby. Some parents who think nothing of spending a small fortune on an outfit that their baby will wear only a few times, are hesitant to invest money in that child's environment. Remember, however, that not only will smart items for your baby's room be used every day for years to come, but that you are creating the backdrop for your child's earliest memories.

GETTING STARTED

Once you have your home organized, think about how the layout of the baby's room will function best. Make sure there is ample storage space for clothing, toys, and books. Avoid basing the nursery decor on overstimulating items. Bright and giant designs on the walls or an abundance of bright flowers over every fabric can be overwhelming. Keep it simple.

CREATE YOUR MAGICAL NURSERY

Time for the fun stuff! After determining the layout of the room, you're ready to start shopping for ideas.

1. LEAD WITH THE CRIB BEDDING. It's best to choose your fabrics first. Your bedding collection will set the stage for the overall feel of the room, so be sure you love it! Build the room out from this focal point so that you are creating a coherent environment.

2. FURNISH WITH NURSERY NECESSITIES. Furniture necessities include a crib; a changing table with two top drawers to store diapers, wipes, creams, and grooming supplies; and an enclosed bottom shelf area for toy and book storage that is easily accessible for floor-time play. An open-style changing table with shelves and storage baskets can also offer easy access to necessities. Choose furniture that fits with your bedding and accessories.

   You will also need a glider with a side table and a child's chair to create a special place of his own. (Once your little one starts crawling, you'll be amazed at how proud he is to climb up in the chair.) Gliders function effortlessly and are much more comfortable than traditional rockers. Whenever possible have all items slipcovered for easy machine-washing. And always select items that are appropriate for the scale of the room.

If you have the extra space, I highly recommend the addition of a twin bed for those nights when your little one is not feeling well and you need to sleep in the room. Think ahead about whether you'll need a trundle bed or even a bunk bed for future siblings if they will need to share the room. Doing this early on with our first baby's room saved us once our fourth arrived.

3. SELECT WINDOW TREATMENTS. Choose something to complement your bedding choice. It's also a good idea to use window coverings flexible enough to make babies accustomed to sleeping in the dark or the light. Roman or pleated shades are good choices.

4. CONSIDER LIGHTING OPTIONS. Overhead recessed lighting gives great coverage for playing and creating. Dimmers are also important for doing midnight diaper changes while keeping baby in sleep mode. Table lamps offer special warmth and add to the beauty of the room.

5. INSTALL CLOSET ORGANIZERS. Having a clean and organized closet for your newborn will help you to keep your sanity after giving birth. You can install organizers yourself or hire a company that specializes in it. Allow for hanging areas, shelving, drawer space, and room for shoes.

6. MAKE GOOD USE OF FLOOR SPACE. If you have wood floors, celebrate them. Not only are they beautiful, but later on it will be fun for kids to have the hard surface for cars and blocks while still having a soft play place on an area rug. When selecting an area rug, choose something that complements your décor and is soft, durable, and easy to clean. If wall-to-wall carpeting is your only option, choose a neutral color and add an area rug to pull the room together and make it cozy.

7. SELECT PAINT. Remember to think calming and soft—almost a whisper of color. And once all of the walls are painted, the color will appear a shade or two darker, so choose accordingly.

8. MAKE SAFETY YOUR FIRST PRIORITY. Make sure all items hanging on walls, such as artwork and peg shelves, are safely hung. Secure the changing table to the wall and the changing pad to the changing table. Window treatment cords should be wound up high out of a baby's or child's reach.

CHOOSE A PEDIATRICIAN

MICHEL COHEN

Dr. Michel Cohen is a pediatrician and founder of Tribeca Pediatrics. He is the author of The New Basics: A-to-Z Baby and Child Care for the Modern Parent.

Choosing a pediatrician is a very emotional process for most parents. You will entrust your most precious treasure to this person, and for this reason the choice should be a careful one. Your pediatrician will be there not only to monitor your child's health, but hopefully to offer you guidance on child rearing, too.

Where to start? Recommendations are the best way to go. Your friends who already have a baby will tell you about their doctors, or, if you are the first one to have kids within your circle of friends, ask around at work or even at the supermarket. When people are satisfied with their pediatrician, they are very forthcoming. Once you have gathered a few names, start with the ones that are geographically convenient and those who participate in your insurance plan.

No matter how good your pediatrician, the care of your baby will be made easier if you are able to get to her office easily. Convenience should not be the only factor, however. If you feel the contact with your pediatrician is not optimal, it is worth looking further to find one with good communication skills and a similar philosophy to yours.

The next step is to set up a prenatal visit to the doctor's office. Most pediatricians make these visits available to prospective parents (usually for free). Go prepared with a list of questions and arrive a few minutes in advance to gather some valuable information about the office, the handling of sick visits, walk-ins, telephone calls, and emergencies. Some offices have separate waiting rooms for sick and well children but this does little for sickness prevention. Most illnesses are contagious at the onset when kids are not yet showing symptoms, and the same staff takes care of both groups of kids, which contributes largely to the transmission of germs in an office.

OBSERVING THE OFFICE

* Look around the office. Is it clean? Are there any cool toys? Is it pleasant? Is it a place where you feel at ease? The décor and the appearance of the office can tell you a lot about the doctor and his philosophy.
* Observe how happy the parents and kids are when they come out of the examination rooms. Strike up a conversation with other parents waiting in the office. You will be able to get a sense of the care and the level of satisfaction from those parents.
* Most important, observe the staff and talk to them. These are the people you will be dealing with at least as much as your pediatrician, so you'll want to get along with them. They are also representative of the work ethic of the practitioner. Are they courteous and accommodating? How do they answer the phone? Are they friendly with parents and, of course, the kids?

THE EXPERTS' GUIDE TO THE BABY YEARS

INTERVIEWING THE DOCTOR

* Ask about office hours. Are there early morning or late evening hours for working parents?
* How long in advance must you book appointments and can you see the same doctor at each visit?
* How are phone calls handled for nonurgent questions and sick visits?
* Does the doctor answer any general questions by e-mail?
* How does the office deal with after-hours emergencies? Find out if they will be handled by your doctor or referred out.
* Is there a twenty-four-hour answering service that can connect you to a doctor? And in what fashion? This is a crucial point.
* Who covers for the doctor when he is on vacation? Make sure that there is a backup doctor so that you are never left in the lurch.
* Ask the pediatrician how much he will guide you in reference to sleep, nutrition, behavioral problems, and child development, and try to gauge his angles on these topics. His expertise is important since most kids are basically healthy and most of the discussions during routine office visits will revolve around these child-rearing topics.
* Last but not least, try to ascertain the philosophy of your future pediatrician with regard to intervention and medications. Pediatricians can be very aggressive in their diagnoses and treatment or have more of a hands-off approach. Although the trend is toward the latter, it is important that you feel comfortable with your pediatrician's approach to medication.

BUY LIFE INSURANCE

BEN G. BALDWIN

Ben G. Baldwin is president and owner of Baldwin Financial

Systems, Inc., a registered investment advisory firm serving

both individual and corporate clients. He is the author of the

best-selling consumer book on life insurance, The New Life

Insurance Investment Advisor, *as well as* The Complete Book

of Insurance *and* The Lawyer's Guide to Insurance.

$\mathbf{B}$ uying life insurance is an expression of love for your baby and your family. We buy life insurance not for ourselves, but for our survivors. Here are the steps to securing the right policy for your loved ones.

1. HOW MUCH SHOULD I BUY?

The question is not how much you need but how much your survivors will need. You've probably heard all sorts of rules of thumb such as buying ten times your annual income, but here is my suggestion: consider the face amount of the life insurance policy as a lump sum of money to be invested after your death to provide a continuing annual income for your family. Although insurance companies will dole out the death benefit in monthly checks, most people wisely take the entire amount in one check with the intention of investing as much as they can after paying off the current bills. Let's assume your family should be able to earn about 5 percent on that invested capital. For example, a $1,000,000 life insurance policy death benefit invested at 5% ($.05 \times \$1,000,000 = \$50,000$) should be able to generate about $50,000 per year for your survivors without eating into the principal. Determine how much income your survivors will need in your absence (e.g., $25,000 per year), and then work backward to buy enough life insurance (e.g., $25,000/.05 = $500,000$), so you would need to buy a $500,000 policy to generate enough income to pay the current yearly bills ($25,000) plus enough to generate the yearly income that will be needed to pay future bills indefinitely.

2. HOW MUCH WILL IT COST?

Don't panic! Term life insurance, the type that does not include any saving or investment element, is incredibly inexpensive these days. The younger and the healthier the insured, the less life insurance costs. Cost also varies with the size (face amount) of the policy and the period of time (term) you want the policy in force. It is easy to go to the Internet to obtain quotes and buy a policy or you can call a licensed life insurance agent. Agent or Internet, the cost should not be much different.

3. WHAT KIND?

All life insurance that pays just the insurance company's money to the beneficiaries is term life insurance. Paying a premium that covers more than the term insurance costs for a life insurance policy is an investment decision. Right now we want the term life insurance activated as quickly as possible so that your beneficiaries are not at risk.

The next decision to be made is what kind of term life insurance to buy. The cost will go up as you extend the time period (e.g., a ten-year term costs less than a twenty-year term, which costs less than a thirty-year term). As long as you buy "convertible" term life insurance to start, you can convert your term policy into another type of life insurance the company offers that contains a savings or investment element.

4. HOW DO I APPLY AND BUY?

You have determined how much insurance you want, what kind, and have an idea about how much it will cost, so it is time to choose a life insurance company to provide your coverage. Choose well-known, highly rated, financially stable insurance companies. Ask the company to provide its ratings and then choose a company with an A or higher rating from three independent rating services. Once you have selected a company, it is time to do the paperwork, give the insurance company a check for the estimated premium, and get a concrete offer from the life insurance company. Writing a check before the application process is complete will put your life insurance in force before the policy is actually delivered so that the risk is taken off your family and shifted to the insurance company as soon as possible.

Expect the application to be long and to include questions about your health, occupation, and avocations. The insurance company may insist on giving you a physical (on its dime). Once it has put together your information, it will offer you a life policy that you may either accept or decline during what is called a free look period of typically ten to twenty days. If the policy does not include everything you want, you can refuse delivery. The insurance company is required to give you all of your money back even though it may have been absorbing the risk (i.e., it would have been obligated to pay some or all of the death benefit had the proposed insured died) during that period of time. Once you have decided to put life insurance in force, do it as quickly as possible.

By purchasing life insurance, you have now seen to it that your survivors will be taken care of economically. Congratulations!

WRITE A WILL

GARY SCHATSKY

Gary Schatsky is an attorney and the founder of Independent

Financial Counselors, one of the first fee-only financial advisory

services firms for individuals. He is chairman emeritus of the

National Association of Personal Financial Advisors and was

selected as one of Worth *magazine's 250 best financial planners.*

A will is your written expression of not only how you wish your assets to be distributed upon your death but also who should be entrusted with raising your children, if they are still minors upon your death. While there are many good computer programs available to help you draft your will, it is best to seek professional guidance to ensure that the will is enforceable in your state and that you have considered all of the issues necessary to protect the interests of your spouse and your child.

A will is essential in ensuring that the plans you make will be both known and followed. Here are the many decisions you will face in creating your will:

GUARDIANSHIP

Clearly financial issues are important, but for new parents, focusing on who will raise your children if you're not around will probably have an even greater impact on their future well-being. While each state has its own rules governing who will raise your child if you die, most courts will honor the "guardian" as named in the parents' wills. The guardian will effectively take over the role of parenting, educating, and caring for your child. This is someone you trust to instill a value system in your child. In only the rarest circumstances, when the court feels that a proposed guardian is not in the "best interests of the child," will your wishes not be followed.

THE EXECUTOR

The executor carries out the wishes you set out in your will, basically deciphering your entire lifetime of financial decisions in a few months. He or she pays your bills, consolidates your assets, and distributes all of what you own according to your wishes in the will. Usually parents select each other as the first choice and then a family member or a professional to serve as the executor should they both pass away. Make sure you have trust in this person both personally and financially, as he or she will make the decisions needed to wrap up your financial affairs.

GIFTS AND TRUSTS

While the majority of wills give most or all of the money to your spouse if he or she is still living upon your death, you'll need to make a more involved decision about what should be done if both of you are deceased. In addition to potential gifts to other family members or charities, most people establish what are known as "trusts" for their children. A trust is a legal instrument that details how assets are to be managed and distributed for the benefit of your children.

The person who manages the trust is known as the trustee. The trustee will be entrusted to manage your remaining assets, so select someone honest who has either the financial expertise to manage money left to the children in the trust or can be counted on to obtain that knowledge from a professional. Finally, you want to be sure that the trustee will share your values regarding your child's welfare.

Often a trustee is given discretion to make distributions for the child's health, education, maintenance, and welfare. You wouldn't want a trustee who would never release any money to your child, nor would you want one who distributes money irresponsibly from the trust. While most trusts allow the trustee discretion to spend money on the child's behalf, they might also have trigger dates upon which they must distribute money. You will need to consider what age your child should be when he gains unfettered access to the money. Often people decide to require distributions at age eighteen, twenty-one, or twenty-five, and anything remaining over the next few years.

Keep in mind that an executor's job is usually completed within months, while a trustee's job could continue for years, depending on the terms of the trust.

While death is likely the last thing you want to think about as new parents, writing a will is a parental responsibility that makes both financial and emotional sense.

PREPARE YOUR RELATIONSHIP FOR PARENTING

GAYLE PETERSON

*Dr. Gayle Peterson is a family therapist and founder of
www.askdrgayle.com, a free online resource for parents. She is
the author of* An Easier Childbirth, Birthing Normally, *and*
Making Healthy Families. *Peterson is a clinical member of the
Association for Marriage and Family Therapy, a diplomat with
the National Association of Social Work, and on the advisory
board of* Fit Pregnancy *magazine.*

With the arrival of your newborn, you and your partner must combine two galaxies, and differing family patterns may sometimes clash under the challenges and stress of parenthood. Each of you will bring strengths and weaknesses to your parenting. Working together as a team to reflect on the past and plan for your future is the beginning of your parenting partnership.

The love you have felt from your own parents may have left you with positive feelings about your own ability to parent. Or you may feel that your parents were lacking in some way, which you want to make up to your own child. It's important to become aware of where your strong feelings about parenting come from. By becoming aware of your own wounds, you can heal without projecting your needs onto your child, and you'll be more likely to form healthy relationships with your children.

It is not the problems that you face that define your success or failure but how you face them! The quiz below will determine where you need to work in order to be a successful parenting team. It allows you to identify the following five major dimensions of a couple's health:

1. How you make decisions
2. Whether you have established a healthy boundary around your relationship
3. Your level of support from family
4. How well you stay connected when you argue
5. The warmth of your connection

Answer the quiz questions that follow separately. Then share your answers with each other to see if there are discrepancies with your experiences in the relationship

1. How often do you complain that your partner does not consult with you about decisions that involve you both?
   1 = always
   2 = most of the time
   3 = 50% of the time
   4 = occasionally
   5 = never

2. How would you describe the way your partner treats his or her parents' suggestions when making a decision?
   1 = partner always takes his or her parents' suggestions over mine

2 = partner always agrees with his or her parents but acquiesces to my point of view if different

3 = partner is overly influenced by his or her parents' suggestions but discusses decisions to be made with me before coming to a conclusion

4 = partner always opposes his or her parents' suggestions

5 = I feel my partner and I work as a team in making decisions for ourselves. His or her parents' suggestions are not an issue.

3. How would you describe your relationship to your partner's parents?

1 = cool and emotionally distant

2 = stifling

3 = overly close

4 = close knit

5 = comfortable and supportive

4. When disagreements occur my partner and I:

1 = get angry and cannot complete discussions

2 = get stuck in a cycle of blaming and withdrawing without coming to an agreement

3 = emotionally shut down and stop talking for at least 24 hours

4 = take some time apart but are able to reconnect and talk about the disagreement within 24 hours

5 = remain emotionally connected through the argument even if we continue to disagree

5. The following ratio best describes how my partner and I verbally express love and appreciation versus complaints and criticism:

1 = 20% love and appreciation to 80% complaints and criticism

2 = 50% love and appreciation to 50% complaints and criticism

3 = 60% love and appreciation to 40% complaints and criticism

4 = 70% love and appreciation to 30% complaints and criticism

5 = 80% love and appreciation to 20% complaints and criticism

SCORING THE QUIZ

There are no right or wrong answers. Add up your score and compare your answers with your partner to see how you fare at this time in the coupling stage.

SCORE OF 20 TO 25

Congratulations. You are both comfortable when it comes to teamwork and honoring the intimacy of your relationship. You both feel successful with making decisions and feeling appreciated by the other. You are able to express warmth and your foundation is strong.

SCORE OF 15 TO 19

Not bad. You are having some conflict around decision making and need to work on developing a style of interacting that makes you both feel considered and comfortable. Your relationship needs some tweaking to be able to handle the stress of parenting.

SCORE OF 5 TO 14

Needs work. If you are not able to resolve conflicts and remain emotionally connected through arguments, your relationship will likely falter under the weight of new parental responsibilities. Work on verbalizing love and appreciation to your partner and learn to disagree without punishing, withdrawing, or attacking your partner. Warm up the atmosphere between you with consistent expressions of love that are not overridden by criticisms.

SCORING DISCREPANCIES

If your questions reflect a feeling of consideration and comfort, while your partner's do not, or the reverse, look out! One of you is not in touch with reality. Remember that it takes two to get married but only one to file for divorce. It is not uncommon for a spouse who does not feel heard by the other to be dissatisfied in a marriage, while the other person discounts his or her concerns, experiencing the relationship as mostly satisfactory.

Make room for feelings without forcing a solution to the problems your partner is sharing with you. Most of the time, partners just want their feelings heard. It's important not to trivialize your partner's feelings that make you uncomfortable. Instead, swallow false pride. Learn to listen without being defensive. Reflect your partner's feelings by playing back what he or she is saying to demonstrate that you understand his or her feelings. Even if you do not agree with his or her conclusions, this will go a long way in releasing emotional pressures so that you can feel connected even if you disagree.

If you determine that you are having trouble with decision making, handling conflict, and keeping warmth, love, and understanding alive in your marriage, counseling could help.

For the ongoing health of your relationship, make time to continue to discuss what kind of parents each of you wants to be and how responsibilities will be shared. Discuss how each of you was parented, and what you do and do not want to repeat and incorporate in your own parenting team. Have several discussions over candlelight dinners at home or talk while you take a walk. Make it your priority to continue these discussions on a regular basis, not only when conflict arises but beforehand. And remember to identify how you might help one another with difficult or painful areas. You are partners on this journey, so you don't have to do it all alone!

8

HELP YOUR CHILD WELCOME A NEW SIBLING

Nancy Samalin

Nancy Samalin is the author of four books, including
Loving Each One Best: A Caring and Practical Approach
to Raising Siblings. *She is the founder and director of Parent*
Guidance Workshops, located in New York City, and has
been conducting workshops for over two decades.

Have you ever wondered why sibling rivalry exists?

Unless you had twins, your first child will be an only child until you bring home "a friend for life." And why doesn't the first child share your undiluted enthusiasm in welcoming a new sibling? Because it's very hard to share someone you love. Most of us are not receptive to sharing our spouses with someone younger and cuter!

With a bit of love and understanding, you can play a big part in helping your child welcome the baby. Here's how to prepare him for the "blessed event" before the baby arrives:

* Don't tell your child how he will feel, such as, "You're going to have so much fun having a baby sister."

* Take your child with you to visit a friend who has a new baby and try to find opportunities to spend time with your child around infants and babies. Let your child see a nursing mother.
* If possible, sign your child up for sibling preparation classes at your local hospital or birthing center.
* Show your child his baby pictures and talk about what his first year of life was like.
* Remind your child that babies can't do much in the first few months so that he won't expect an instant playmate.
* Mention all the things he can do as a toddler or preschooler that babies are unable to do.
* Teach your child to practice gentleness by playing with a pet, a doll, or his favorite stuffed animal.
* Involve your child in preparing for the new arrival by having him draw pictures for the baby, help you pick out names, and go with you when you buy baby clothes.

   Once the new baby arrives:

* Give your child many opportunities to help you with the baby. He can hand you diapers, try to make the baby laugh or coo, and play baby games such as peek-a-boo.
* If your child wants to hold the baby, have him do so while sitting on the floor so that he won't let the baby fall (or "accidentally" drop the baby).
* Don't leave a toddler or preschooler alone with an infant or young baby. Sometimes what starts out as a hug can end up as a stranglehold!
* Listen nonjudgmentally if and when your older one expresses negative feelings about the baby. If your three-year-old son complains,

"All she does is cry and poop," you might respond, "Yes, I can see the baby sometimes annoys you."

* Set limits on behavior. Your older child can't be permitted to hurt the baby, but do be permissive with feelings such as jealousy. He may have a hard time sharing you and having less of you and your spouse to himself.

* Spend time alone with your older child, making him the focus of your attention. To make the time more meaningful, use a phrase when describing it, such as "my special time with Jeremy," so your child can look forward to having you all to himself.

* Avoid comparing your kids throughout their childhoods. Celebrate each one's uniqueness.

* Don't futurize: "Oh, my son is so hostile toward my new daughter. Will they ever be friends?" Remember, the only constant between siblings is that their relationship is always changing.

9

PREPARE YOUR PET FOR BABY'S ARRIVAL

NANCY PETERSON

Nancy Peterson is the companion animals issues specialist

for the Humane Society of the United States.

You're probably wondering how your first "baby," your pet, will react to the new arrival in your home. Just as people do, pets like routines. Knowing what to expect and when helps them feel safe. No doubt, the arrival of a new baby will upset the daily routine for you and your pet. The best way to help your pet adjust is to gradually introduce changes before the baby arrives, such as putting baby powder on your body to get your pet used to the scent or familiarizing your pet with baby-related objects. Whether or not that occurred before you brought Baby home, you'll want to consider these suggestions:

* Take your pet to the veterinarian for a routine health check. Discuss any pet health or behavior issues that concern you and would cause you to restrict interaction between your baby and your pet.

* Spay or neuter your dog or cat. Sterilized pets are calmer and have fewer health problems associated with their reproductive systems.
* Redirect pet behaviors such as nibbling or swatting at you and others toward appropriate objects.
* Accustom your pet to regular nail trims.

When you return from the hospital, your pet may be waiting, eager to greet you and receive your attention. It's a good idea to have someone else take the baby into another room while you give your pet a warm, but calm, welcome. Keep some treats handy so you can distract your pet from the baby.

It's up to you to model appropriate behavior for your child and to understand the following:

* Pets need space and may not always welcome human attention, especially when eating, playing with their toys, or resting. Provide pets with a place of their own where they can retreat from children.
* Animals may become upset by too much petting or stimulation. Warning signs (such as hissing, lip curling, retreating, and growling) indicate that pets want to be left alone.
* Don't put your pets in situations where they feel threatened; these may include being stared at, cornered, or hugged.
* Teach children not to pull the animal's tail, ears, or other body parts, and insist that they never tease, hit, or chase the pet. When they're old enough, teach children how to properly pick up, hold, and pet the animal.

Allowing children to help care for a pet teaches them responsibility and instills in them a feeling of competency and accomplishment. Although certain pet-care activities must be handled by adults, you can still include your children by explaining why and what you're doing. With supervision, toddlers can help care for an animal friend by selecting a new toy or collar, assisting with grooming, or carrying food.

Ultimately, your children will learn how to treat animals—and people—by watching how you treat the family pet. They'll study how you feed, pet, and exercise your companion animal. And they'll pay close attention to how you react when a pet scratches the furniture, barks excessively, or soils in the house. Frustrating as these problems are, "getting rid of" the pet isn't just unfair to the pet and your children, but it also sends the wrong message about commitment, trust, and responsibility.

May you pass on *your* fond memories of a beloved childhood pet to the newest member of your family.

10

PREPARE FOR BABY'S ARRIVAL HOME

SANDY JONES

Sandy Jones is the author of eight books on pregnancy,

parenting, and child care. Her newest books, co-authored with

her daughter, Marcie Jones, are Great Expectations: Your

All-in-One Resource for Pregnancy and Childbirth *and*

Great Expectations Pregnancy Journal and Planner.

T here's a lot to do when it comes to getting your "nest" ready for little Junior.

CREATE A HEALTHY ENVIRONMENT

If you decide to go all out in the nursery department, plan to fix up your little darling's room well in advance of your due date. Doing the painting, wallpapering, and carpet laying months ahead will allow toxic fumes time to evaporate before your baby arrives with his sensitive lungs. You can speed up the air-clearing process by opening windows and using an exhaust fan or by running a dehumidifier with a built-in air filter.

All of your baby's bedding and clothing should be washed in advance to remove dust and the residues of dye chemicals. The best detergents for washing both baby bedding and clothing are nonallergenic, perfume-free brands.

SETTLE THE SLEEPING LOCALE

Most new parents prefer to keep their baby in the same room with them, at least for the first month or two. You can bring in a miniature crib or bassinet on wheels. These can be rolled out of the bedroom when you want privacy—something you can't do with big cribs.

DEAL WITH DIAPERS

Diapering is an action you'll do countless times before your baby graduates to "big kid" pants. In the meantime, use a water-resistant pad on your bed or floor, or select a wooden changing table with high sides and a belt to hold Baby safely in place while you do the "dirty" work. You'll also need a method of disposing of the diapers until the garbage truck arrives, such as an odor-resistant, self-sealing diaper pail with a supply of liners, or a tall trash can with liners. (Reusable diapers will need a pail for soaking with a self-locking lid.)

Before Baby's arrival, buy at least four packages of disposables in the "newborn" size. You can buy more later. Most parents like having a box of diaper wipes and a package of refills, too.

SELECTING DOCTORS AND SUPPORT

You'll need to choose a pediatrician for your baby well in advance of the birth. The pediatrician can help you make your circumcision decisions ahead of your boy baby's arrival. You may also want to explore having a postpartum doula (postnatal care assistant) or baby nurse to help you with basic baby care and breastfeeding after you bring the baby home.

PARENT PROOFING YOUR HOME

There's no need to go to great extremes to babyproof before you bring your baby home. Instead, "parent proof" your home by making a clear runway that allows you to get around without tripping in the days when you're carrying your baby all the time. Install nightlights *in every room* for visibility when on night duty.

Finally, two important grandmotherly pieces of advice are worth remembering: "This, too, shall pass," and "The stores will still be open after your baby arrives."

11

SELECT AND INSTALL A CAR SEAT

JENNIFER HUEBNER

Jennifer Huebner is a certified child passenger safety instructor and manager of Traffic Safety Programs for AAA, North America's largest motoring and leisure travel organization.

Now is the time to make your vehicle safe for Baby with a properly installed child safety restraint. Regrettably, vehicle crashes remain a leading cause of death for children in America. This is not only an immense tragedy but one that is—in many cases—preventable. When used correctly, car seats are effective in reducing injuries and fatalities for infants and toddlers.

SELECTING A CAR SEAT

Naturally, you want to choose the seat that will be the safest for your child. The good news is that all child safety seats on the market are required to meet the same federal motor vehicle safety standards. When selecting the perfect seat, choose one that fits your child, your vehicle, and your budget.

It is important to always read the child safety seat manufacturer's instructions and your vehicle owner's manual to determine the correct location and proper installation procedures for your vehicle. In the United States approximately eight out of ten car seats are installed improperly. The most common mistakes are seats that are not installed tightly, harness straps that are too loose, and harness retainer clips that are not at the proper level.

BASIC GUIDELINES

Be sure to keep your infant in a rear-facing seat until age one *and* at least 20 pounds, when he will be ready for a forward-facing seat. An infant has a very fragile head, neck, and spine. Rear-facing seats are designed to absorb the crash forces along the seat's shell, cradling your infant in an accident.

REAR FACING

* Ensure that the seat is at the proper angle and it is snug; you should not be able to move the seat more than an inch in any direction when testing at the belt path (where the seat belt routes through the car seat).
* The harnesses should be adjusted to slots at or below your child's shoulders, without twists, and should be snug so you cannot pinch any slack. The harness retainer clip should be placed at armpit level.
* Additional padding is discouraged as it may interfere with the way your seat is designed to perform in a crash. Accessories also may become potential missiles in your vehicle during a crash or sudden stop. These include mobiles, toys, attachable mirrors, roller shades that attach via suction cup, tissue boxes, books, purses, umbrellas, and anything in the vehicle that is not secured. Keep such items in your trunk.

FORWARD FACING

* Your forward-facing seat should be installed in an upright position, according to manufacturer's instructions. As with a rear-facing seat, you should not be able to move the seat more than an inch in any direction when testing at the belt path.
* The harnesses should be adjusted just as with a rear-facing seat (see the previous page).

THE NEXT STAGE

A common misconception is that once a child outgrows the forward-facing child safety seat, he or she is ready for a seat belt. Seat belts were designed with an adult male in mind and can be dangerous for small children. The lap belt can ride up on a child's abdomen and cause abdominal injury, and shoulder belts can cut into the neck. Instead, use a booster seat to help properly position the seat belt on your child. Make sure the booster allows the lap portion of the belt to stay low across your child's hips and upper thighs, and that the shoulder belt is positioned across the sternum and collarbone.

Your child may ride in a lap-and-shoulder belt when the belt fits properly. Proper fit means your child is able to sit with his or her back against the vehicle seat and knees bending at the edge of the seat without needing to slouch. The lap portion of the belt should remain low across the hips and upper thighs, and the shoulder portion of the belt should remain across the sternum and collarbone for the entire trip.

Visit www.nhtsa.gov for a list of certified child safety seat technicians to help with installation. You are now on the road to ensuring that your child's journey is a safe one!

12

BABYPROOF

DEBRA SMILEY HOLTZMAN

Debra Smiley Holtzman is a child safety advocate and the author
of The Safe Baby: A Do-It-Yourself Guide to Home Safety.
She was a Reader's Digest *"Everyday Hero" and was named a*
"Woman Making a Difference" by Family Circle *magazine.*

M ore than 4.5 million children are injured in the home every year. By following these simple prevention measures and closely supervising your children, you can help protect them from common household hazards.

Look for hazards from your baby's perspective. Get down on your hands and knees and crawl around the room. You will be surprised by what you see!

PREVENT CHOKING, SUFFOCATION, AND STRANGULATION

* Remove small objects from your baby's sight and reach. Choking items include batteries, coins, small balls, balloons, hard round foods, and removable rubber tips on doorstops.
* Lock up or remove suffocation hazards such as storage chests and latch-type freezers. The best choice for a toy chest is one without a lid or with a lightweight removable one.

* Repair or replace corded window coverings purchased before 2001 (when design standards changed) and keep all chains and cords out of your child's reach to prevent strangulation. Better yet, get cordless window treatments.
* Buy a new crib that meets current safety standards. Corner posts should not extend more than $\frac{1}{16}$ inch above the end panels. Larger extensions can cause entanglement with clothes. Distance between crib slats should be $2\frac{3}{8}$ inches or less to avoid entrapment.
* Remove all soft, loose, and fluffy bedding from the baby's sleep area. This includes pillows, comforters, bumper pads, and stuffed toys. Place your baby on his back to sleep.

PREVENT FALLS

* Install window guards on all windows from the ground floor up. A child can fall from a window that is opened more than 4 inches, and screens offer no protection. Use quick-release mechanisms for fire exits.
* Position cribs and low-standing furniture away from windows.
* Use safety gates at the top and bottom of stairs. Do not use a pressure gate at the top. Such a gate can give way if a child leans on it.
* Avoid scatter rugs. If used, add a nonskid backing or place a nonskid mat underneath them.
* Use angle braces or anchors to secure to the wall any large or heavy objects that might tip over (including appliances, dressers, bookcases, and entertainment centers).
* Store heavier items on bottom shelves and install safety latches to keep children from opening drawers and climbing on them.
* Place lamps, TVs, and other entertainment equipment on sturdy, low furniture, and set them as far back toward the wall as possible.

Remove freestanding items, such as floor lamps and breakable knickknacks.

* Attach corner and edge protectors to all sharp furniture edges to cushion the bumps and falls.
* Check for recalled products and stay up-to-date by visiting www.recalls.gov.

PREVENT POISONING

* Store household cleaners, medicines, vitamins, alcohol, and other potentially poisonous substances in their original containers, locked up and out of sight and reach of your child.
* Remove poisonous plants.
* Install a carbon monoxide alarm in every sleeping area and place one at least 15 feet from any fuel-burning appliance. Have fuel-burning appliances inspected by a professional annually.
* Test your home for lead-based paint if it was built before 1978.
* Prominently post emergency numbers near every phone.

PREVENT BURNS AND CUTS

* Set your water heater to 120 degrees F. Water at a temperature of 140 degrees F will produce a third-degree burn on a child in just 3 seconds. Be aware that 120 degrees F can still burn your baby, so always mix hot water with cold water before it touches your child's skin. A comfortable water temperature for a child is near his own body temperature, 98 to 100 degrees F. Never exceed a temperature of 100 degrees F.
* Use back burners and keep pot handles turned to the back of the stove.
* Keep hazardous items such as sharp utensils, lighters, matches, and other flammables locked away.

* Install smoke alarms on every level of your home and in every sleeping area. Change batteries once yearly; test them monthly; replace the units every 10 years. Plan escape routes and conduct fire drills with the entire family.
* Place safety covers over all unused electrical outlets and power strips, and replace frayed cords.
* For lighting rooms where a toddler roams, a ceiling light fixture or a wall lamp is best.
* Keep electrical appliances away from sinks or tubs.
* Install ground fault circuit interrupter (GFCI) outlets around any source of water.
* Use a fireplace screen in front of any open flame and install a switch lock on gas fireplaces.

PREVENT DROWNING

* Install locks on the toilet and store all buckets upside down.
* Immediately empty water from a tub, sink, or container after it has been used. A baby can drown in as little as 1 inch of water.
* Never leave a child unattended in or near water, even for a second.
* Install four-sided isolation fencing, at least 5-feet high and equipped with self-closing and self-latching gates, around a home pool or spa.

Remember, babyproofing can never be 100 percent effective. Proper supervision is always required.

13

BREASTFEED

CORKY HARVEY AND WENDY HALDEMAN

*Corky Harvey and Wendy Haldeman are co-founders of
the Pump Station, providing lactation classes and support
services for new parents from their two locations in Los Angeles.
They are faculty members of the UCLA Lactation Educator
program and serve on the advisory board of Fit Pregnancy.*

T hough we know that breastfeeding is important, this natural act remains difficult. In many cases, our mothers did not breast-feed and now that extended family members typically don't live with younger generations, fewer of us are surrounded by support-ive, experienced women to mentor us. This means that we come to breastfeeding with little experiential knowledge and, often, very little hands-on help. Making milk is physiologically normal and happens naturally if we manage our breastfeeding appropri-ately, but the knowledge and skills of breastfeeding must be learned. The following suggestions should help make your expe-rience easier and more rewarding.

TAKE A PRENATAL BREASTFEEDING CLASS WITH YOUR PARTNER

Learn about common roadblocks and solutions, normal newborn behavior, deep latch-on technique, and how to tell if a baby is getting enough. To be supportive, those surrounding you should also understand breastfeeding, so have them attend class as well. Choose an excellent teacher. Ask your doctor, childbirth educator, and friends for recommendations.

START RIGHT AWAY, STAY TOGETHER, AND NURSE OFTEN

Babies usually remain alert for an hour after they are born and are ready for their first feed. Immediate skin-to-skin contact keeps the baby warm and facilitates the first latch. Research has shown that mothers and babies who stay together right after birth initiate breastfeeding more easily and have fewer problems.

Keep your baby with you all the time so you can feed on demand. Don't wait for the baby to cry. Instead, watch for feeding cues such as mouth and eye movements, wiggling, and little noises. Newborns should nurse eight to twelve times every twenty-four hours, with one three-hour sleep stretch and at least one three-hour wakeful period during which the baby will nurse very frequently (cluster feeding). When an infant sucks at the breast, a message is sent to your brain, and hormones are released that cause the breast cells to produce and release milk. The more your baby suckles, the more milk you will make.

LATCH DEEPLY

This part is mechanical at first but soon becomes so easy that you won't even think about it. If the infant's latch is shallow, a mother's nipples can become damaged and painful, so it is important that your baby's mouth cover the areola or at least most of it. An infant's lower jaw is quite recessed yet needs to be placed well behind the nipple for proper latching. To achieve this, place your hand behind the baby's head with your thumb near one ear and your index finger on the other. Compress the breast with your free hand making it a bit flatter. Now tip the baby's head back by pressing between the shoulder blades with the heel of your hand. Let his or her chin touch the breast. Place your nipple just above the baby's upper lip and wait for the baby to open very wide. Let the lower lip drag all the way as you now bring the baby's upper jaw over the top, nose to the breast. This allows the nipple to land deeply on the baby's tongue. Release the breast after the baby is latched. You are putting the baby on the breast, not the breast into the baby's mouth: an important difference. If the baby has 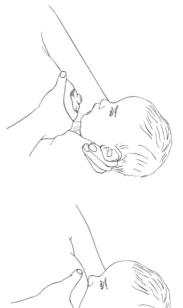 latched on correctly, you should feel a pulling/tugging sensation but not severe pain. Break the suction and try again if you feel the latch is incorrect.

DON'T SUPPLEMENT

The leading cause for discontinuing breastfeeding in North America is a woman's belief that she has an inadequate milk supply. This is a misconception. Almost every woman can make enough milk for her baby. Supplementing with formula leads to an unfortunate downward spiral: the less the baby feeds at the breast, the less the mother will be stimulated to produce milk, and the supply will plummet.

PROTECT YOUR MILK SUPPLY

Frequent nursing best protects your milk supply, but mothers sometimes have to consider other options when a baby is unable to nurse or latch on to the mother's breast. In these cases, a woman must express the milk from her breasts eight to twelve times every twenty-four hours in order to maintain a good milk supply.

HOW TO TELL IF YOUR BABY IS GETTING ENOUGH

You can tell a baby is getting enough milk if the baby swallows when nursing; urinates six times and has at least three loose, yellow stools every twenty-four hours by six days old; is satisfied after most feeds; and regains birth weight within two weeks.

GET HELP

Before giving birth, know where to go for breastfeeding help. Ask every nursing woman you meet for her recommendation. Also check with doctors, midwives, nurses, childbirth educators, and breastfeeding teachers. Numerous moms before you have struggled during the first weeks and have overcome breastfeeding problems such as sore nipples, low milk supply, inability of the baby to latch on, engorgement, and overproduction. You, too, can overcome these obstacles.

14

BOTTLE–FEED

LORAINE STERN

*Dr. Loraine Stern is a clinical professor of pediatrics at
UCLA and has been in private pediatric practice for
thirty-five years. She is the author of two books on child care
and co-editor of the* American Academy of Pediatrics Guide to
Your Child's Nutrition. *She has been a contributing editor
to* Woman's Day *magazine for twenty years and is a
former editor of* Healthy Kids *magazine.*

Although there is no question that "breast is best" for your infant, there are a variety of reasons why a mother may not nurse. She may need medication that would be harmful to the baby. She may have had breast surgery that makes it impossible. Some women are devoted breastfeeders but have to return to work and are not able to pump and store milk easily. Other women just do not want to breastfeed. Whatever the reason, bottle-feeding can provide complete nutrition and be fulfilling for both mother and child.

WHICH FORMULA SHOULD YOU CHOOSE?

All of the commercially available formulas have adequate nutritional content. They are all slightly different, however. If there are no close relatives who have had serious milk allergies, any of the major milk-based formulas will do. The issue then is price. The major formulas are more expensive, and some have higher levels of docosahexaenoic acid and arachidonic acid (commonly known as DHA and ARA, respectively), fatty acids that are thought to contribute to eye and brain development. These will be listed on the label. If money is an issue, the less expensive ones, which are lesser known probably because they do not spend millions on advertising, are just fine.

If there is a history of severe allergy to cow's milk in any close relative or asthma or eczema, a formula that is not based on cow's milk might be appropriate. Soy-based formulas are the traditional alternative, but some children react to soy as well. Formulas such as Nutramigen or Alimentum contain proteins that are predigested into smaller molecules and are less likely to provoke reactions. Rarely, a child is so allergic to a formula that hives, vomiting, or severe abdominal pain occurs almost immediately. In most cases, however, milder forms of formula intolerance such as diarrhea, poor weight gain, or excessive gas or constipation take a few days to develop. If your child is allergic to soy or develops symptoms of formula intolerance ask your pediatrician to recommend an alternative formula.

WHAT BOTTLES AND NIPPLES SHOULD YOU USE?

Do not buy a truckload of one kind of bottle and nipple just because one of your friends swears by it. Every baby is different and you cannot know what your infant will prefer until you start feeding him. For some infants with a small mouth, the shorter, curved nipples are better. For infants that are smaller than average or were premature, sometimes a softer nipple with a larger hole for faster flow is better. When your child is old enough to hold her own bottle, one with an indented middle may be easier for her to hold. Buy a few different ones and see which your baby likes best.

HOW DO YOU RECOMMEND PREPARING THE BOTTLE?

Some infants need their formula warmed; others do not seem to care. If you do warm a bottle, it is best to do it in warm water rather than in the microwave so that you don't risk uneven temperatures burning the baby's mouth. Test the temperature by dropping some on the bottom of your wrist. If the milk is about the same temperature as your skin, it is fine.

If you have a dishwasher, you do not need to do an elaborate sterilization process. Just running the bottles and nipples through a hot cycle and letting them air dry is enough. Bottled water is okay, but good, clean city water is adequate, too. If you are on a well, be sure the water is not too high in some minerals. Your water company should supply you with the numbers and you can check with your pediatrician. Do not reuse a bottle that has formula left in it. The enzymes and bacteria from the baby's mouth can spoil the milk quickly.

WHAT IS THE RIGHT WAY TO BOTTLE-FEED?

Hold your baby just as you would if breastfeeding—close to your chest with a pillow under your arm or resting your arm on the soft arm of a chair or sofa. Baby should drink with his head elevated slightly—not bolt upright or horizontally but at about a 15-degree angle. This prevents milk from flowing into the back of the nose and throat, which can lead to ear problems or choking. Never let your infant lie flat on her back to drink and never prop a bottle. Once a child can hold her own bottle she can also remove it from her mouth when she chokes, but propping the bottle up into her mouth can make the situation worse.

Do not let your child take a bottle to bed and fall asleep drinking it. This can lead to "nursing bottle cavities." Milk sitting in the mouth decays the teeth and will cause expensive and traumatic corrective dental procedures later.

WHAT ABOUT BURPING?

Infants need to burp but you do not have to dedicate your life to it. Spending about 10 minutes with your baby in different positions to try to bring up a burp is adequate.

Finally, do not feel guilty if you choose to bottle-feed. Millions of children have grown up strong and healthy on formula.

15

RECOVER FROM A C-SECTION

Rita Rubin

Rita Rubin covers women's health for USA Today.

She is the author of What If I Have a C-Section?

Y ou've just had a Cesarean section? Join the club. More American women than ever before are delivering via C-section. As you've probably gathered by now, a C-section is major abdominal surgery. To complicate matters, you have a newborn—and perhaps a toddler and/or older sibling waiting at home—to care for.

Repeat after me: "I can't do it all." Let your husband change the baby's diapers. Graciously accept your neighbor's offer to make dinner. Ignore the dust bunnies that are reproducing like mad under your bed, or better yet, pay someone to eradicate them.

On average, it takes about six weeks to feel close to normal after a C-section. Some women speed through their recovery in less time, but others may take longer.

BREAST IS BEST FOR BABY AND YOU

Breastfeeding is best for your baby, and research suggests it might help your incision heal more quickly. Experiment with different positions to find one that's comfortable. At the very beginning, try lying on your side, tummy to tummy with your baby. But soon you might prefer the traditional cradle hold, as long as a pillow separates your baby from your still-tender incision.

HE AIN'T HEAVY; HE'S MY BABY

If you attempt to lift anything heavier than your baby, you could be setting yourself up for a hernia. Ditto for stretching to reach an item on a high shelf—that's what step stools are for—or climbing the stairs too much. Trying to rise out of a too-soft chair can also strain your incision. Instead, park yourself on a firm, straight-backed one for a while.

TO DRIVE, PERCHANCE TO SLEEP

Sleep deprivation and painkillers, not to mention distracting thoughts about your newborn, may interfere with your ability to focus on the road, at least for a week or two after a C-section. When you feel ready to get behind the wheel, let someone else ride shotgun and judge how you're doing before you go solo.

NOT NOW, DEAR . . . I HAD A C-SECTION

Sleep, not sex, may be the only bedtime activity you're up to right now, and it's probably just as well. Most doctors advise women not to have sex for at least six weeks after giving birth, whether vaginally or by C-section. If you were in labor, it takes that long for the cervix to close. An open cervix, and all the blood and gunk flowing through it, predispose you to a uterine infection if you have sex. (Remember, even if you deliver by C-section, you still need a plentiful supply of maxi-pads to soak up your vaginal discharge after birth.) If your C-section incision hasn't had a chance to heal, pressure on it during sex could also increase your chances of developing a uterine infection.

YOU GOTTA WALK BEFORE YOU CAN RUN

Even when you were still in the hospital, the nurses probably got on your case about getting out of bed and walking to prevent postsurgical blood clots and muscle stiffness. No matter what shape you were in prior to your pregnancy, you should hold off on aerobic exercise until six weeks after your C-section. That goes for abdominal crunches as well, and if your abdominal muscles separated during pregnancy—a condition called diastasis recti—you'll probably have to wait eight weeks or so. In the meantime, you can perform Kegel exercises to reduce your risk of incontinence down the road: tighten the muscles around your vagina and rectum as though you have to do number one and number two but the nearest bathroom is miles away.

EVEN C-SECTION MOMS GET THE BLUES

A few studies in the early to mid-1990s suggested that women who delivered by C-section were more likely to suffer from postpartum depression than other new moms, but more recent research found no such connection. Still, if your baby is a few months old and you're still feeling down because you didn't have your ideal birth, talk to your doctor about getting counseling or finding a support group for women who've had C-sections.

16

PROTECT BABY FROM HARMFUL GERMS

PHILIP M. TIERNO JR.

Dr. Philip M. Tierno Jr. is the director of Clinical Microbiology and Diagnostic Immunology at New York University Medical Center. He is an associate professor in the Departments of Microbiology and Pathology at New York University School of Medicine. Tierno is the author of several books, including The Secret Life of Germs: Observations and Lessons from a Microbe Hunter.

Germs are a normal component of our body; there are ten times more germ cells in our bodies than there are body cells. Although humans emerge from the womb sterile (i.e., germ free), as the baby passes through the birth canal, or makes contact with the mother's body, he picks up a "germ passport," a complement of microbes that will seed the growth of normal germ flora (good germs) that will protect the baby. As a child grows and matures, his body chemistry changes, making it hospitable to an even fuller array of good germs at various bodysites. This process begins the most important part of the development of a healthy immune system for baby and it is also an opportunity for you to help reduce the risk of infection in your child.

YIN AND YANG

We have learned to coexist with germs quite well. There is, however, a yin and yang to germs. On one hand, good germs guard the entry points of our body from infection, help us with digestion of food and provide nutrients like vitamin K, and, most important, are critical to the proper development of a healthy immune system. On the other hand, germs can make us sick. When it comes to germs, the state of health and well-being depends on the balance between good and bad germs.

RISK OF INFECTION

Because children typically have poorly developed immune systems they are most at risk for infection. Eighty percent of all infections are spread via direct (like kissing) and indirect (touching doorknob) contact. The other 20 percent of infections are spread through the three other modes of transmission: vector borne (e.g., ticks/Lyme disease), common source (such as contaminated food or water), and airborne (like tuberculosis or sudden acute respiratory syndrome).

Below are some ways to reduce the risk of infections:

IN NEWBORNS

1. Breastfed babies fare best. This is so even for low-birth-weight babies, who develop fewer infections and allergies than bottle-fed babies because mother's milk contains antibodies and other valuable substances.
2. Healthy newborns should be bathed only with plain tap water (without use of a washcloth) for the first month because their delicate skin is coated with a lipid-rich protective secretion that Baby

receives from the womb. This protects the skin from intruding germs; hence it should not be washed off with soap.

3. Leave the umbilicus open to air to heal without the use of antiseptics (unless it becomes infected).

4. Always wash your hands before (and after) handling Baby whether you have just handled a pet or come in from work or the outdoors. Remember that 80 percent of all infections are transmitted via touch.

5. Keep sick children or adults away from newborns.

IN TODDLERS

1. As children grow into toddler stage their immune system gets a boost from the many vaccinations they receive. Most modern vaccines are thimerosal (mercury)-free but check with your pediatrician to be sure.

2. If possible, avoid use of child-care or nursery settings. In such environments children easily pass potential disease-causing germs to other children and adults. If not possible, make certain the facility has good hygiene practices in place, including an isolation area for ill children.

3. In day-care and preschool settings children are at significantly greater risk for diarrheal illness. Diaper changing is probably the greatest single means of contact transmission of germs to caregivers, teachers, other children, and family members. Always wash hands after diaper changing.

4. Sanitize stuffed animals periodically by putting them in a hot dryer.

5. Clean hard toys with soap and water or 3 percent hydrogen peroxide; if grossly contaminated with urine, feces, or vomit, use mild bleach solution to disinfect; rinse well and air dry.

GOOD HYGIENE

Teach children good hygiene so they can learn to protect themselves. Teach them the following practices:

1. Wash hands before eating or drinking and after using toilet facilities.
2. Never use someone else's eating or drinking utensils (even their best friend's).
3. Never eat food that has fallen to the floor.
4. Practice good cold and flu etiquette, such as covering one's mouth and nose during a sneeze or cough.

17

DISTINGUISH HEALTHY VERSUS SICK SIGNS

TANYA REMER ALTMANN

Dr. Tanya Remer Altmann is a pediatrician at Community
Pediatric Medical Group in Westlake Village, California,
and a clinical instructor at Mattel Children's Hospital at
UCLA. She is a spokesperson for the American Academy
of Pediatrics and is editor in chief of the Academy's new child
development parenting book, The Wonder Years.

New parents worry plenty about their baby's health—but in most cases, the baby is perfectly normal. Here are some tips for knowing when you should worry and when you can relax.

TROUBLE FEEDING

I often hear from moms who are concerned that their newborn falls asleep during a feeding. It helps to undress her down to her diaper or change the diaper before a feeding to wake her up. See your pediatrician if you're still having difficulty, if she isn't feeding at least every four hours, if her skin has a yellowish color (jaundice), or if she's not making wet diapers.

STOOLS

It's either too much, too little, or not the right color and it really freaks new parents out. But babies poop in a wide variety of colors, consistencies, and frequencies. After birth, stools are brownish black in color and then lighten to brown, green, and yellow over the first two weeks, in that order. They also change consistency from thick and sticky to seedy and looser. You may think he's developing a pattern and then out comes a green one, or a looser one, or on one day there isn't a dirty diaper at all. Any of these scenarios is okay. If your baby hasn't gone in a few days, his tummy is swollen and hard, or there is blood in the stool, call your pediatrician.

DIARRHEA

Normal infant stools are soft and a little runny, so it's not always easy to tell when a young baby has diarrhea. Look for a sudden increase in frequency or excessive amounts of liquid in the stool. If the diarrhea persists after a few diaper changes, touch base with your pediatrician. Little ones can get dehydrated very quickly so your pediatrician might recommend extra fluid or a change in diet.

SPIT-UP

All babies spit up. Some spit up after every feeding. This occurs because the valve above the stomach is floppy and allows food to easily flow back up (a condition called reflux). So buy a dozen burp cloths and keep them everywhere. Reflux usually resolves by age one. As long as your baby is gaining weight well and the spit-up doesn't bother her, we usually don't treat it. Giving smaller, more frequent feedings as well as burping her and holding her upright after a feeding will help. Call your pediatrician if the spit-up is projectile or forceful, contains blood, is greenish, or if your baby's belly looks swollen or feels hard.

RAPID BREATHING

Babies normally breathe faster than adults, and their breathing rate varies. They may breathe rapidly for a few minutes, pause, and then resume a more normal breathing pattern. Be on the lookout for consistent breathing of more than sixty beats a minute or if the skin between or below the ribs is sucking in deeply with every breath. If these occur or if she seems to be working very hard to breathe or is making funny noises, see your pediatrician. Often it's simply a stuffy nose that's bothering your little one. If that's the case, put a drop of saline in each nostril and gently suction the mucus out.

SLEEPINESS

Newborns actually sleep a lot, just not through the night as we'd like. In the beginning it may seem as though he's sleeping all day, but as long as he wakes up every few hours to eat, that's fine. As your baby gets older he'll have more awake time during the day and longer sleep periods at night. If he is sleeping noticeably more than usual, isn't waking up to feed, or is rarely alert, call your pediatrician.

EXCESSIVE CRYING

Babies cry! When they're not sleeping, eating, or pooping, they're crying! They cry when they are hungry, wet, cold, hurt, or for no apparent reason at all. If he's been fed, burped, changed, and checked to make sure nothing is hurting him, it's okay to let him cry for a little while. Often it's just his way of blowing off steam. If he's truly inconsolable, call your pediatrician.

SKIN

Most infants have dry, flaky skin that may start to peel after the first day—you would, too, if you had been soaking in fluid for nine months! They also have a wide variety of rashes, bumps, spots, and even acne. Don't worry, having baby acne doesn't mean more acne as a teen. Most are normal newborn skin conditions and will go away with time—no treatment needed.

Initially, babies don't have good circulation so bluish hands and feet or mottling (pale lacey pattern) of the arms and legs can be normal. The skin should "pink up" as the area is warmed. If the bluish color persists or appears in other areas such as the lips or mouth, let your pediatrician know.

FEVER

A temperature over 100.4 degrees is considered a fever, which signals that there is an infection. *An infant under two months of age with a fever should see a doctor as soon as possible,* as she can get very sick very quickly.

EYES

A blocked tear duct is very common in the newborn period. Most of the time this will resolve as your baby grows. If it is still present around one year of age, a pediatric eye doctor may need to dilate the duct with a simple probing procedure.

All babies receive antibiotic eye ointment in both eyes after birth to prevent infections. Sometimes an infection can occur later, though, especially in babies with blocked tear ducts, and may require antibiotic eye drops. Signs of an eye infection are yellow or green eye discharge, red eyes, and any redness or swelling around the eye.

By no means is this all that will worry you during the newborn period. Never hesitate to call your doctor if you feel something is wrong. After all, that's what we pediatricians are here for—even at 4 A.M.!

18

REDUCE THE RISK OF SIDS

FERN R. HAUCK

*Dr. Fern R. Hauck is an associate professor of family medicine
and public health sciences at the University of Virginia
Health System. She is a member of the American Academy
of Pediatrics Task Force on Sudden Infant Death Syndrome
and a leading SIDS researcher.*

B abies sleep a lot, so creating a safe sleeping environment for babies is just as important as keeping them safe when they are awake. Sudden infant death syndrome (SIDS) and accidental suffocation can occur during sleep. SIDS is the sudden death of an infant that remains unexplained after an autopsy and review of the medical history and circumstances of death. The risk of SIDS is about 1 in 2,000 births in the United States. It is most common among infants two to four months of age but can occur at any time in the first year of life. While there are no guarantees as to how to prevent SIDS and accidental suffocation, these guidelines will help you do your best to protect your baby:

1. PLACE YOUR BABY ON HIS BACK TO SLEEP. Since doctors introduced the recommendation to place babies on their backs for sleep over ten years ago, the number of SIDS deaths has declined by more than half. Always place babies on their backs for sleep, whether at night or for daytime naps. The side position is less stable and should not be used because babies can role onto their stomachs from this position, increasing their risk of SIDS. To help prevent changes to the shape of the head, alternate the end of the crib on which the baby is placed for sleeping, as babies will turn toward the direction of activity and sound. Limiting time in carriers, car seats, baby swings, and bouncy seats will help prevent head flattening as well. Babies will also need "tummy time" during the day under adult supervision to help with motor development.

2. USE A FIRM MATTRESS. Place babies to sleep on a firm mattress in a safety approved crib or bassinet. Remove any soft or fluffy objects from the baby's sleep environment, including pillows, sheepskins, comforters, stuffed animals, and thick, pillowlike bumper pads.

3. SLEEP IN THE SAME ROOM BUT NOT IN THE SAME BED. It is safer for babies to sleep in their own crib or bassinet in their parents' bed room than in bed with their parents. Studies have found that infants who sleep in the same bed with their parent(s) are at increased risk of SIDS as well as accidental suffocation deaths. It is not known exactly what the mechanism is for this increased risk of SIDS. Having the crib or bassinet close to your bed will make it easier to bring your baby into bed for feeding and cuddles and to place the baby back when you are ready to sleep. Some people worry that avoiding bed sharing for sleep may interfere with breastfeeding. You don't have to share a bed to successfully nurse

your child. Never sleep with a baby on a couch or chair, even for naps, and do not allow other children to sleep with the baby. These activities are too risky—they increase the risk of SIDS and accidental suffocation.

4. AVOID SMOKE EXPOSURE. Keep babies free from smoke exposure. No one should smoke in the same house or car as the baby.

5. PREVENT OVERHEATING. Babies don't need to wear more clothing than adults. Keep the room temperature comfortable and use only a thin blanket or a sleep sack. If using a blanket, keep it from covering your baby's face by tucking it into the sides and end of the crib. It is best to place your baby "feet to foot"—that is, Baby is placed near the foot (end) of the crib, so that the blanket can be tucked in more easily at the end and sides of the mattress.

6. OFFER A PACIFIER AT BEDTIME. Offer your baby a pacifier when going to sleep at night or for naps. If you are breastfeeding, wait three to four weeks before introducing pacifiers to make sure that nursing is well established. The evidence continues to mount that the risk of SIDS is greatly reduced when infants use a pacifier for sleep. A leading theory suggests that pacifiers may increase an infant's arousal (ability to wake up easily) during sleep and influence other autonomic functions.

7. GET REGULAR CHECKUPS AND IMMUNIZATIONS FOR YOUR BABY. Babies need to be seen for regular well-child checkups and immunizations. Seek medical attention if your baby becomes ill. Be sure to discuss SIDS guidelines with your medical professional as well.

8. BE CONSISTENT. Babies do best with a regular routine. It is recommended that you follow these SIDS guidelines consistently and let everyone who cares for your baby know about them also.

As a parent, you have many decisions to make. Hopefully, these guidelines will help you—and your baby—rest a little easier.

19

PREPARE FOR AN EMERGENCY

MARK WIDOME

*Mark Widome is a pediatrician and professor of pediatrics
at the Penn State Children's Hospital. He is a former chair
of the Council on Child and Adolescent Health of the
American Academy of Pediatrics. He is a regular
contributor to NBC's* Today.

E mergency situations happen relatively infrequently with babies, but parents should be prepared, because decision making in true emergencies can save a life.

FEVER AND SEIZURES

Fever is only a symptom, not a disease. As worrisome as it might be, a fever serves the useful purpose of jump-starting the immune system to better fight infection. In infants and young children, a fever can get quite high but, contrary to popular myth, not so high as to cause brain damage or any other serious harm. The myth leading to parental "fever phobia" results in part from the common occurrence of brief seizures with high fever in about 2 percent to 4 percent of infants and children between the ages of six months and five years. The correct emergency response to a febrile seizure (i.e., one that's caused by fever) is to simply keep your infant comfortable, remove excessive clothing, and sponge him with tepid water. If the seizure lasts more than five minutes or interferes markedly with breathing, call 911. Infants with high fevers—with or without seizures—usually need to be evaluated by the pediatrician the same day to determine that the cause is not a serious infection.

BREATHING PROBLEMS

The choices are relatively straightforward if your baby develops problems breathing. If breathing problems are part of an illness or infection (wheezing or croup), then your infant needs to be seen by the pediatrician promptly for assessment and treatment. Depending on how hard your infant is working to breathe, you may be advised to go directly to the hospital emergency room rather than the doctor's office. On the other hand, your pediatrician may offer home telephone advice for mild symptoms.

Usually, sudden breathing problems in an infant who is not ill arise from choking. If your child is coughing, offer encouragement to him, because no first-aid measure is more effective than a good strong cough. If your child is experiencing too much blockage to cough, follow the instructions for "back blows" and "chest thrusts" that you learned in your infant first-aid or basic life-support course. The course is a must for you to take.

HEAD INJURIES

Most infants take at least one significant fall in the first year. Pediatricians like to say that "babies bounce well," yet sometimes it's hard to tell whether a blow to the head is more than minor. Go by how hard the hit to the head seemed to be—did she fall onto soft carpet or down the steps?—and how your baby is acting once the expected crying stops. Be concerned if she does not seem alert and normally responsive, if her pupils are not of equal size, or if she has repeated vomiting or is lethargic. In all cases, at least a telephone call to the pediatrician is in order.

BURNS

Scald burns (from hot water or coffee) are more common than contact burns (touching the toaster). For scald burns, immediately remove any hot, wet clothing, and for any burn, immediately hold the burned part under cold running water for at least five minutes to cool the skin. This can significantly reduce the depth and seriousness of a burn injury. Call your doctor for all blistering burns larger than a quarter or for *any* burn on the face, hands, or genital area. Burns should be treated with an over-the-counter antibiotic ointment such as Bacitracin and covered with a loose "nonstick" bandage. Large burns can be temporarily covered with a clean disposable diaper, if a large sterile bandage is not immediately available.

POISONING

Anything that your infant swallows that is not food is potentially a poison. That includes medicines, houseplants, household cleaning supplies, cosmetics, and chemicals. In all cases, if there is any doubt, call the regional poison information center for timely advice at 800-222-1222. Don't give your child syrup of ipecac. Prevention tip: know the botanical names of your houseplants, so the poison center can advise you accurately if your child ingests part of one.

FINAL ADVICE

Most emergencies can be prevented. Childproof your home systematically. Take a first-aid or basic life-support course. Post important phone numbers—the doctor, the poison center, the hospital emergency department—or enter them in speed-dial so you can find them when you need them. And, finally, think through common scenarios and how you would respond. Most parents show good instincts in emergency situations, just as they do in the everyday nonurgent tasks of raising a child.

20

IDENTIFY AND TREAT COLIC

Barry Lester

Dr. Barry Lester is director of the Brown Center for the Study of
Children at Risk, Brown Medical School and Women and
Infants Hospital, which houses the Colic Clinic. He is also
professor of psychiatry and human behavior and pediatrics at
Brown Medical School and the author of Why Is My Baby
Crying? The Parent's Survival Guide for Coping with Crying
Problems and Colic.

Crying is normal. Colic is not. People who trivialize colic not only are wrong but are also doing a huge disservice to families who have colicky babies. Downplaying the condition just makes those parents feel like there is something wrong with them as caregivers.

SYMPTOMS

Colic is a crying disorder that affects family function. It occurs when there is a persistent pattern of crying that is more frequent and more severe than is typical for newborn babies *and* the crying results in impairment in other areas of function.

Signs of disordered crying include the following:

* The baby is crying too much or too often.
* The baby may show sudden onset of colic episodes during which time the baby is inconsolable.
* The sound of the cry may change and become high pitched and loud.
* The crying may include long periods of breath holding.
* There may be physical signs such as stiffening of arms and legs, legs being pulled up to the stomach, stomach tight, fists clenched, and/or the face turning red.
* The baby may act like and sound like he or she is in pain.

Clear evidence of impairment in other areas may occur:

* The crying could affect the baby's general development or other behaviors, the two most common being sleeping or feeding.
* The behavior could affect the parent-infant relationship by resulting in attachment or bonding problems.
* The behavior could affect the family function, causing stress in the marital relationship. Parents may feel inadequate, suffer a loss of self-esteem, and feel ineffective. They may feel angry and disappointed that their baby is acting this way.

A crying, irritable baby can set up a vicious cycle, in which Baby, Mom, and Dad are miserable.

TREATMENT

It's important to know that colic is a problem affecting not only the infant, but the family as well. The first step in treatment is helping parents understand that they did not cause the colic. The second step is to determine the root cause of the colic. Sometimes the colic is related to another behavioral disorder, which, when treated, can reduce or eliminate the colic. For example, a baby may be thought to have colic, but the primary problem turns out to be a sleep disorder. Or the baby may be experiencing a medical problem, such as reflux, which can be treated with medication. Other times it is just the baby's internal physiology kicking its heels and has nothing to do with other problems. In this case, we use strategies for soothing and calming, like massage, providing more or less stimulation depending on what the baby likes, changing to a cow's-milk-free diet if bottle-feeding, or restricting Mom's diet if she is breastfeeding.

At the same time we determine how the colic (whatever the cause) is affecting the family and we treat that, too. This involves helping parents understand colic and the feelings it engenders and giving the parents counseling as we determine what issues they face, such as feeling inadequate and helpless as parents, disappointed that they can't "help" the infant, maternal depression (which occurs in 45 percent of colic cases), marital issues, and family dynamics. In other words, we treat the crying, but we also repair the parent-child relationship.

Once you recognize that colic is an identifiable crying problem, treatment becomes not only possible but effective.

For more information on calming a crying baby, see page 75. For more information on massaging a baby, see page 141.

21

CALM A CRYING BABY

HARVEY KARP

Dr. Harvey Karp is the author of two DVDs and two best-selling books, The Happiest Baby on the Block *and* The Happiest Toddler on the Block. *He is an assistant professor of pediatrics at the UCLA School of Medicine.*

Caring for a new baby requires love, patience, and the skillful completion of two main jobs—feeding and calming the baby's crying. Those who succeed at both tasks feel on top of the world. But those who struggle with either end up feeling terrible!

Feeding babies is usually pretty easy. Soothing, however, can be a big challenge. It's not that crying is bad. It's actually a brilliant way for helpless babies to get our attention. But 50 percent of babies fuss more than one hour per day, and their screams can be as loud as a one-hundred-decibel power mower—four inches from our ears! That barrage can make many new parents crumble, and it provokes exhaustion, nursing problems, marital conflicts, even depression.

Fortunately, some simple tips can turn anyone into a world-class baby calmer!

First, you need to know that in many ways our babies are born three months too soon! Unlike baby horses, able to run on their first day, our newborns are smushy little creatures who must be born early so that their big-brained heads don't get stuck in the birth canal. Believe it or not, babies rarely cry from bad tummy pain (even though that's what everyone's told). They actually cry because the world is too quiet and still!

For centuries, moms have known that babies calm fastest when they're held, rocked, and shushed, but until recently no one realized that those things imitate the baby's fetal environment. In the womb, babies enjoy snug holding, jiggly motion, and a constant, whooshy sound of blood pulsations—louder than a vacuum cleaner. Stillness may soothe us adults, but it's sensory deprivation for babies, often driving them bananas.

It turns out that imitating the uterus settles babies because it activates a reflex that all babies are born with—the calming reflex. Reflexes can be a little tricky. For example, the knee reflex works every time you hit the exact spot. However, if you're off by a half inch, nothing happens! Similarly, the calming reflex, this blessed "off switch" for crying, is easy to activate as long as you imitate the womb exactly right. Here are five easy ways to do this—the five S's:

1. *Swaddling:* Snug wrapping is the cornerstone of calming, the essential first step in pacifying fussy babies. Swaddling duplicates the soft caresses babies feel during pregnancy. Your baby may initially struggle against the wrapping, but once he calms it will keep him from flailing and upsetting himself. Use swaddling just for fussy periods and sleep. (Avoid loose blankets around the face and overheating. They have been associated with SIDS.)
2. *Side/Stomach Position:* The back is the only safe sleeping position. But it's the worst position for soothing crying because it can

trigger a feeling of falling. Lay your baby down on his side or stomach; this position cancels that falling feeling and switches on the calming. Once your baby calms and you put him down to sleep, be sure he's on his back.

3. *Shushing:* Strong shushing is "music to your baby's ears." Shush as loudly as she's crying. Then, as she settles, gradually lessen the intensity to about the level of the noise of a shower. (A CD of womb sounds, or a white noise machine, is an invaluable tool to calm your baby's fussing and increase her sleep.)

4. *Swinging:* All infants love movement, but crying babies need fast, ultra-small jiggly motions (back and forth . . . like a shiver). Swings, slings, and rocking chairs help, too. But never jiggle your baby when you're upset or angry.

5. *Sucking:* This wonderful S lulls babies into profound tranquillity. Always offer your fussy baby milk first. Breastfeed if you can— and avoid pacifiers until the nursing is well established because babies use a different style of sucking when using a pacifier.

Soothing your infant is like dancing together—but let him lead! The vigor of your S's should mirror the vigor of his fussies. Dads make supergreat baby calmers because they're usually more comfortable than moms doing snug swaddling, strong shushing, and jiggly swinging. After your baby's crying abates, lessen the vigor and gently guide your swaddled little child to a "soft landing."

Now you're ready to have some fun! And if your baby cries, just look at it as an opportunity to hone your skills and turn your little fusser into the happiest baby on your block!

P.S. Besides quickly calming crying, the combination of swaddling and strong white noise all night should keep the calming reflex switched on and may add a wonderful one to two extra hours to your baby's sleep!

22

SWADDLE

ANDREA SARVADY

Andrea Sarvady is the author of Baby-Gami:

Baby Wrapping for Beginners.

Close your eyes and imagine that you're a fearful newborn, bombarded with strange sensations and unanswerable questions: Where am I? Who are these strange people peering down at me? Did anyone *ask* if I wanted to be named Prescott Lionel Warrington the Third?

It's easy to see how safe refuge from all that might resemble your mother's womb—dark, cozy, and nowhere near the digital camera. This is why swaddling a newborn is a great way to give him or her a terrific feeling of security. A snug wrap looks constricting to us, but feels like a big hug to that tiny, out-of-control body.

We can't promise that perfecting a basic wrap will stop a screaming colic cry, although it has been known to happen. But a good wrap will certainly make your little one easy to carry and safer to pass around when all those eager hands start grabbing for your baby.

Your many new receiving blankets will come in handy right about now. And don't stop wrapping just because your newborn has a growth spurt; babies enjoy a looser version of the snug wrap well after two months. Switch to baby blankets with a little stretch for a quick swaddle as those little limbs outgrow their first soft covers. (We do recommend stopping the swaddle well before preschool, however—no one wants to be laughed off the playground.)

Ready to wrap? It's a snap! Just follow these simple steps:

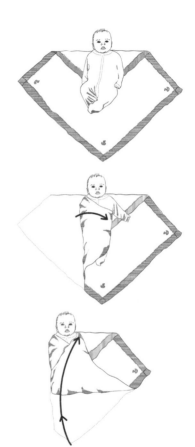

1. Whether your blanket is a square or a rectangle, place it on a flat, comfortable surface in a diamond shape. Now take the top tip of that diamond and fold it down about 6 inches.
2. Lay your baby on his back, head just above the fold and shoulders just below.
3. Holding the baby's right arm at his side so it doesn't move, pull the top right corner of the blanket tightly down diagonally across his body, tucking the material under the left buttock and lower back. Next, while holding the blanket against the left hip, grab the area by the left shoulder and pull it firmly to remove any slack.

4.   Making sure your baby's arms are safely at his sides, pull the bottom corner up and tuck it behind his left shoulder. Note that with some blankets, the material won't stretch that far; if that's the case, you can always tuck it into a **V** at the neckline.

5.   Tuck the bit of material at the top right in and out of the way. Now it's time to use the left side of the fabric to encircle Baby in swaddling heaven. Pull this left end around Baby's body, just like a belt, tucking the last little bit of fabric in at the **V** by the right of Baby's neck.

This basic snug wrap takes a little effort the first time or so, but in no time you'll be wrapping like a master.

Quick tip: When you swaddle a baby, pull the material tighter than you might think is comfy—a newborn craves snugness the way a new parent craves sleep. Yet there is a helpful rule of thumb here: You should just barely be able to slide your hand between the blanket and your baby's chest. Any tighter than that and you have reason to worry, but much looser and your efforts will be futile.

Snug as a bug in a rug? That's your baby!

23

CARE FOR BABY'S PENIS

CARA FAMILIAN NATTERSON

Cara Familian Natterson is a pediatrician with Tenth Street

Pediatrics in Santa Monica, California. She is the author of two

books, including Your Newborn: Head to Toe: Everything

You Want to Know About Your Baby's Health Through the

First Year.

How you care for your baby boy's penis will vary depending on whether or not he is circumcised.

UNCIRCUMCISED PENIS

There are two important things to know: the area under the foreskin never needs to be cleaned, and the foreskin never needs to be pulled back. Debris will almost inevitably collect under the foreskin. It may look like cheesy discharge coming from the opening of the foreskin or it can consolidate lower down the shaft, appearing like a small bump the color and size of a pearl. All of this is normal and there is nothing you need to do about it. Although tempting, it is important not to clean underneath the foreskin because you do not want to force the foreskin back over the head of the penis. This may sound benign, but it can cause big problems, particularly if the opening in the foreskin is small. If the head of the penis swells a little bit, the foreskin can become stuck. Instead of sliding up and down the shaft easily, it bunches beneath the head of the penis, causing more swelling because blood cannot drain properly. This makes it even more difficult to pull the foreskin back to its appropriate position. This can ultimately lead to a condition called paraphymosis, swelling that can completely interrupt the blood supply to the penis. Paraphymosis can necessitate emergency circumcision—probably not the outcome you desire since you have chosen not to circumcise your child in the first place.

The foreskin will move more easily by the time your child is three or four years old. And don't worry if your son moves his own foreskin as he pulls on his penis later in infancy and toddlerhood. You shouldn't manipulate your child's foreskin, but it's not dangerous if he does.

CIRCUMCISED PENIS AND POSTCIRCUMCISION CARE

Most circumcisions are performed in the first two weeks of life, many of these in the first few days after birth, before you and your baby leave the hospital. Regardless of when the circumcision is performed, the after-care is fairly standard.

Removing the foreskin leaves the head of the penis exposed. It may look raw and ooze some blood. The penis generally heals very quickly. Most people who perform circumcisions—like doctors and moyels— recommend covering the head of the penis with a lubricant like Vaseline or vitamin A and D ointment in the twenty-four hours following the circumcision. Alternatively, you can soak a gauze pad in Vaseline, creating a mini-bandage that will self-adhere when soaked. If gauze is applied, it will fall off within twenty-four hours of the procedure.

These salves provide a water-repellent material so that your baby's urine and stool will not stick to the newly exposed skin. This keeps the area relatively clean, speeds healing, and reduces the chance that the healing skin will stick to the diaper. Continue lubricating the area for about a week after the circumcision. After applying a thin layer of ointment to the head of the penis, you can wipe the excess on the inside front of the diaper, further reducing the likelihood of sticking.

Sometimes as it heals, the head of the penis will look red. Other times, it may be spotted with white or yellowish patches. This is called granulation tissue. It is a normal part of the healing process. If the head of the penis looks purplish, call your doctor. Also contact your doctor if oozing continues following the twenty-four hours after the circumcision or if the area begins to bleed actively.

Once the circumcision has healed, there is very little long-term care required. Sometimes the skin along the shaft of the penis just below the circumcision rides up, sticking to the lower part of the head of the penis. This is called an adhesion. If your child develops adhesions at any point during the infant or toddler years, you may use a lubricant (like Vaseline) and gently pull down on the shaft skin, slowly separating it from the head of the penis once or twice daily for several weeks before it resolves completely. If you are unsure about whether your child has adhesions and to discuss proper treatment, check with your doctor.

24

RECOGNIZE POSTPARTUM DEPRESSION

KAREN KLEIMAN

Karen Kleiman is a psychotherapist and founder and director of the Postpartum Stress Center in Pennsylvania. She is the author of several books on postpartum depression, including What Am I Thinking? Having a Baby After Postpartum Depression.

Everyone promised you that this would be the best time of your life. But instead of feeling pure joy, you may find your feelings are more complicated. Maybe you're overwhelmed, exhausted, or weepy. Maybe you're wondering why you decided to have a baby right now. Or perhaps you miss your old life and wish you could go back to who you were before the baby came. Some of these feelings are normal, especially right after birth. So how do you know if your feelings are actually a sign of something more serious like postpartum depression (PPD)?

Here are some things to keep in mind:

* PPD is not the baby blues. The blues are characterized by feelings of sadness, weepiness, anxiety, guilt, or inadequacy.

They are common (85 percent of all new mothers experience them), last for a few days after birth, and require no treatment.

* Postpartum depression is a potentially serious complication of childbirth that affects 10 percent to 15 percent of women. If you are feeling blue for more than two weeks after birth or if your symptoms also include anxious thoughts, difficulty sleeping (when it isn't because your baby is keeping you up!), change in appetite, panic, and/or scary thoughts of harming yourself or your baby, you might have PPD.

* PPD is a clinical depression that usually occurs within the first three months, but it can arise anytime within the first postpartum year or even beyond.

* PPD is a real, medical illness. It is not your fault.

* Women with PPD typically say things like, "I just don't feel like myself" or "I'm afraid I will never feel better" or "I'm afraid to tell anyone how I really feel."

There is a common myth that women with PPD always feel detached from their babies or have terrible thoughts about hurting themselves or their babies. Mothers will say, "I can't have postpartum depression, I love my baby too much." In fact, some women with PPD feel anxious and depressed but are still very attached to their babies. Others may feel nervous, confused, and afraid to be alone with the baby, or they may be ambivalent.

The symptoms of PPD can be very frightening and this fear can inhibit women from seeking the help that they desperately need. What's most important is that you get a proper diagnosis and treatment.

What should you do if you suspect you might be suffering from PPD?

Trust your instincts. Women are typically very good at sensing when something isn't right. If you have a gut feeling that something isn't right or the way you feel scares you, you need to take action. *(If your symptoms are severe, or if you are having thoughts of hurting yourself or your baby, let your doctor know immediately or have someone take you to an emergency room.)*

Initiate self-care. New mothers often neglect to take care of themselves. Taking care of yourself physically is an important foundation.

* Eat well, and avoid caffeine and alcohol.
* Sleep when you are able.
* Rest when you can't sleep.
* Get out in the sun.
* Exercise if you can.
* Spend time with people who make you feel good.

Reach out. Talk to your husband or partner. Let people who are close to you know how you are feeling and what you need from them. Accept help from others and protect yourself by not overdoing it. Do not let embarrassment or shame get in the way of taking care of yourself.

Let a professional know. Find the provider that you feel most comfortable with, whether it is your OB-GYN, midwife, family doctor, psychiatrist, or therapist. Let someone know how you are feeling so you can initiate treatment, which generally consists of supportive psychotherapy and antidepressant medication, if your symptoms warrant it.

PPD is a common, frequently unrecognized, yet complicated disorder. It is very treatable. The keys to recovery are early identification and intervention. With proper support, education, treatment, and time, you will feel better again.

25

GET IN SHAPE AFTER CHILDBIRTH

Pamela Peeke

Dr. Pamela Peeke is the author of the best-selling books Body
for Life for Women *and* Fight Fat After 40. *She is an
assistant clinical professor at the University of Maryland School
of Medicine and an adjunct senior research fellow at the
National Institutes of Health. Peeke is the chief medical
correspondent for Discovery Health TV.*

The glorious event has happened: Baby is here—along with a
lot more fat on your body. Most women heed doctorly advice
and keep the pregnancy weight gain within twenty-five to thirty-
five pounds. Even though you probably quickly shed ten to fifteen pounds postpartum, all women are left with fat on their
bodies. Jelly bellies, thunder thighs, bodacious buttocks, and
bountiful breasts are precious remembrances of Baby's past
lodging in what used to be your svelte prepregnancy figure.
Don't worry: you can shed those last pounds whether you've just
given birth now or two years ago.

The first step is to quit obsessing about weight. You're missing the point. Your goal is to minimize your body fat and maximize your muscle tone. Fat occupies four times as much space as muscle so your dress size is up from prepregnancy even if you are back to your normal weight, and each pound of muscle—the body's main calorie-burning engine—cooks thirty-five to fifty calories a day versus five to ten for fat. Pitch the scale and buy a body composition analyzer. It looks like a scale and costs about the same. Your body fat percentage goal is between 20 percent and 25 percent. Adult women with less than 20 percent body fat are genetically skinny, competitive athletes, or medically ill.

Keep in mind that breastfeeding is a dandy way to reduce fat in your hips, thighs, and buttocks. Baby needs 400–600 calories from breast milk every day. A woman's postpartum hormones help mobilize those delectable calories for Baby. The result? Fat removal and slimmer legs and behind. It's a terrific win-win.

My Mind, Mouth, and Muscle template will also help you achieve your body composition goal. First, the *Mind*. It's time for a new postpartum mantra: "I am no longer eating for two." Your pregnancy ménage à trois—you, Ben, and Jerry—has got to stop. Your new mental focus is the transition to a postpartum routine of healthy eating despite the interrupted sleep and daily challenges of managing a newborn.

Now, the *Mouth*. Watch for portion distortion, read food labels, and keep to the recommended serving sizes. What you overeat and don't burn off, you wear. Finally, science has shown that if you eat a balance of smart foods—highest-quality carbohydrates (50 percent), fats (25 percent), and proteins (25 percent)—every three to four hours, you'll achieve and maintain the best body composition.

Muscle means burning those calories up. Buy a pedometer and measure your steps each day. Your goal is to reach at least 10,000 steps per day, which is equivalent to a little over four miles. That's 5,000–7,000 more steps than the average woman takes each day. Be patient as you ease back into physical activity. If you had an uncomplicated vaginal birth, you can start walking right away and reach your 10,000-step goal within four weeks. If you had a C-section, give yourself eight weeks to reach your goal.

Read your pedometer and you'll see that every step counts—literally. Get chunks of walking in throughout the day. Walk at least five minutes every hour if you have a sedentary job. Use the walk/jog stroller as often as you can. Walk the dog; walk after or before each meal during the day. Take the stairs; avoid the escalator and elevator.

To tone your muscles, you can start to lift light weights twice a week starting at week 6 (or week 8 for C-sections). Do core training to get control of your postpartum pooch. Mix it up with yoga and Pilates.

A final note about age: If you're thirty-five years or over, getting back into shape will take longer. Just stay persistent and consistent and you'll achieve a positive postpartum mental and physical transformation, and sustain it—for life.

26

REDUCE AND ELIMINATE
STRETCH MARKS

HOWARD MURAD

Dr. Howard Murad is the founder of the Murad Skin Research

Laboratory and creator of Murad skin-care products. He is an

associate clinical professor of dermatology at UCLA. He has a

private practice in El Segundo, California, with a patient base

of more than 50,000 people. Murad is the author of three books,

including The Cellulite Solution: A Doctor's Program for

Losing Lumps, Bumps, Dimples, and Stretch Marks.

The joy of pregnancy is often marred by the aggravation of stretch marks. Fifty to 90 percent of pregnant women experience them to some degree. While the majority of stretch marks are found on the lower abdomen, they can also appear on the thighs, hips, buttocks, breasts, and arms, especially in the last trimester.

Stretch marks occur when there is damage to the middle layer of the skin (the dermis) and the upper layer of skin (the epidermis). This damage results when skin is constantly stretched with growth, as it is during weight gain or pregnancy. Healthy skin contains strong cells that are bouncy and full of water and healthy connective tissue comprising collagen and elastin. It is the elastic middle layer that gives shape to the skin. Once stretched beyond its normal capacity throughout pregnancy, these cell walls break apart, similar to a rubber band that has been stretched out over time. The skin loses its elasticity and the connective fibers break, which shows through the surface as rippled formations, causing the water that keeps the fibers firm and buoyant to spill out.

To prevent stretch marks from appearing, you need to strengthen these layers of skin by simply supplying your skin with the raw materials it needs to fend off damage and repair itself once damage has been done. We need to supplement our diets with enough lecithin and lipids to enable our bodies to maintain firm and intact cells that will keep our skin smooth. Fortunately for our skin, these nutrients are readily available.

Lecithin is a substance found most predominately in soy (e.g., in edamame, tofu) and eggs (whole with yolk), although smaller amounts are found in tomatoes, cauliflower, spinach, and potatoes.

The best lipids to fortify your cell walls are in the family of essential fatty acids (EFAs). Not only do these healthy fats help rebuild your cells, they also attract lost water back into them to help keep them firm and buoyant. Excellent sources of EFAs are olive oil, canola oil, and especially cold-water fish such as sardines, mackerel, and salmon. Because of mercury concerns, women who are pregnant or breastfeeding should limit their mackerel and salmon intake to once every two or three weeks. And note that EFA supplement tablets, found in any health food store, are the safest and surest way to get your daily allowance.

You'll also need to address stretching in the dermis. The raw materials needed to repair it are glucosamine and amino acids, the building blocks of proteins such as collagen and elastin. Glucosamine gives skin its bulk and firmness. It is not readily available in any food source, so it must be taken as a supplement. Collagen and elastin are the main tissues of the dermis, giving skin its elasticity, and their breakdown is a prime culprit in skin conditions such as wrinkles, cellulite, and stretch marks. To prevent this breakdown, your best sources of protein are nuts, beans, fish, and lean meat.

If stretch marks have already appeared, address them soon after birth with topical and internal care. Keep up a well-balanced diet with plenty of these nutrients, and you will be seeing smoother skin in a matter of weeks.

STRETCH MARK TIPS

BEFORE AND DURING PREGNANCY	AFTER PREGNANCY

Keep skin moist. Look for hydrating ingredients, such as aloe, vitamin E, ceremides, sodium PCA, hyaluronic acid, shea butter.

Maintain a healthy weight that is appropriate for your body type and recommended by your physician. Maintain a healthy diet that is full of fresh fruits and vegetables (1 cup four times daily) along with healthy fats such as olive oil, flax seeds (1 teaspoon), nuts (6–10 nuts) and nut butters (1½ teaspoons). Total fats = 3–4 servings daily.

Avoid excess sun exposure before, during, and after pregnancy. Ultraviolet rays weaken the skin's collagen and elastin fibers.

Begin using products that encourage cell turnover, such as glycolic acid, lactic acid, retinol (available over the counter in cosmetic formulations), or tretinoin (prescription only).

Stimulate circulation with ingredients such as cayenne pepper and tiger's herb.

Support skin internally with dietary supplements that contain EFAs (taken in 1 g fish oil or flaxseed oil capsules with 600 mg of borage seed oil), glucosamine (1,200 mg), antioxidants, and anti-inflammatories.

Lasers can be helpful. Have a consultation with a qualified physician to understand the options.

27

PACK A DIAPER BAG

KATE SPADE

Kate Spade is the designer of Kate Spade New York, a collection of handbags, diaper bags, shoes, accessories, and home products sold worldwide. In the fall of 2005, she extended her collection of baby products. Spade is also the author of a series of three books entitled Occasions, Style, *and* Manners.

It sounds like it should be straightforward: a bag for diapers. But a diaper bag represents the portable repository of a parent's anxieties; it's a glorified first-aid kit, assembled to meet the needs of a small child venturing from the nest into the wild. For this reason, most diaper bags are far too complicated, both in their construction and in their contents. When your little one is crying, you want to eliminate her discomfort immediately, not dig past umpteen books, lotions, and bags of Cheerios, through five pockets, for a pacifier that's usually near the bottom. For the sake of your sanity, your spinal health, and (last but not least) your fashion sense, keep your diaper bag simple.

1. PACK LIGHT. Overpacking usually happens when you allow sheer exhaustion to make you lazy. You're not paying attention, so you don't realize you're not using half of what you've put in there. Unless your child is an early and avid reader, the collected works of Beatrix Potter will just weigh you down. And unless your child has an abnormal metabolism, those four bottles and ten diapers are just taking up space.

   An everyday bag needs only the following: four diapers (my baby and I are never away from home long enough to need more than two—the other pair are for psychological comfort), a pacifier, ointment, antibacterial hand wipes (for grocery-store cart handles, dropped toys, and anything else she might pick up), sunscreen, a bottle of formula or water, clean socks or booties, and a cloth diaper for wiping up spills or spit-up. Rattles or musical toys might staunch tears, but they annoy the heck out of anyone within hearing distance, so forgo those. (Let's face it, most babies can be entertained by a stray teaspoon.) If your baby is a little older and needs more developed diversions, include a soft rattle or a cardboard book that can double as a chew toy. Lastly, include an emergency phone list so that if something happens to you, someone else can get your baby's other nearest and dearest on the phone immediately.

2. DON'T RESTOCK YOUR BAG RIGHT BEFORE LEAVING THE HOUSE. You'll be too likely to overpack under pressure. Instead, do it when you have a calm, quiet moment and can focus on what you both really need. Keep your bag stocked at all times.

   A corollary to this rule: have a larger, separate bag for airplane or long car trips. In this one you'll want to include doubles of what you've got in your everyday bag, at least two meals, a change of clothes (pack separates as opposed to one-piece gear, because it's easier to dress a baby in a top and a bottom when you're in public), a blanket, and a kit that includes any necessary medicine, teething gel, and a thermometer. When I travel with my kids, I usually forgo my purse to accommodate all this stuff, so my travel diaper bag is big enough to fit my magazines and lip balm, too.

3. GO FOR A RUDIMENTARY DESIGN WHEN BUYING A DIAPER BAG. A balance of chic and practical is ideal. Gender-neutral is good, too, since your partner will want to carry it without feeling silly. As far as colors or prints, go with what pleases you and blends easily with your purse or briefcase. It should be disguised as a handbag; there's no reason to shout "diaper bag." Think durable and dark colored. A tote, shopper, or messenger-style bag is the easiest to get in and out of, and its shoulder straps should be long enough for you to reach into the bag with one hand without having to put it down. Bring your stroller with you when you shop for it, so you can make sure your bag fits easily over the handle. One or two internal pockets are good for the small items you grab most (like a pacifier), but those pockets should be easily accessible from the bag's main opening.

A diaper bag is primarily about ease and convenience. The more time you spend out with your baby, the better you'll know exactly what you both need. In the interim, less is more.

28

PREVENT AND TREAT
DIAPER RASH

STEVEN P. SHELOV

Dr. Steven P. Shelov is chair of the Pediatrics Department and

vice president of Maimonides Infants and Children's Hospital of

Brooklyn. He is the editor in chief of Your Baby's First Year.

Suddenly you notice that your precious young infant has red-ness on her bottom. Don't worry: it is easily treated and will respond to the simplest remedies, and even though it may return, it usually disappears for good once your baby gets older. Most likely, what you are seeing is a diaper rash. Most often, this rash includes redness or red bumps just in the area of the diaper. It can extend up onto the lower abdomen but is often reddest on the thighs, genital area, and other areas that have been in direct con-tact with the baby's wet diaper. Diaper rash is most visible in young infants and often in eight- to ten-month-olds whose diets are expanding. As more foods are introduced, their digested prod-ucts can be irritating when they come out in the bowel movement.

The causes of this common irritation are frequently one or both of the following:

* A wet diaper has been left on too long, allowing the moisture to make the skin more susceptible to chafing. Once the area is chafed, substances in the urine may cause further irritation.
* A diaper is left on the baby with stool in it for too long. This may expose your baby's sensitive skin to the acidic nature of digested foods in the stool, which can further irritate the skin.

Along with the domino effect of irritation, the area may also become infected with a yeast called Candida, if the irritated skin is not protected. In addition, when stools are looser or more frequent, such as during diarrhea, or when the baby is on antibiotics, the diaper rash can become particularly irritated.

To prevent and treat diaper rash:

* Change the diaper as soon after the bowel movement as possible.
* Change wet diapers as frequently as possible; five to eight times per day is not too often.
* When feasible, especially if you see the start of diaper rash, or if the baby already has it, leave the diaper off and the diaper area exposed to the air.
* Use a Vaseline-type protective ointment, such as Desitin or A&D, to cover and protect the irritated area. Reapply the ointment during every diaper changing.
* Add an anti-Candida cream, on advice from your pediatrician, if your baby develops Candida rash, often recognizable by a cluster of raised dots on pink skin as opposed to the redder, more spread-out diaper rash.

Rest assured, this little annoyance will disappear as you learn to recognize the simple diaper rash and stay on top of preventative strategies.

29

PRACTICE GOOD DIAPERING ETIQUETTE

TRISHA THOMPSON

Trisha Thompson is executive editor of Wondertime. *She is a former editor in chief of* Babytalk *magazine and has worked as an editor and writer for* American Baby, BabyCenter.com/ParentCenter.com, *and* Parenting.com. *From 1999 to 2005 she wrote "Reality Check," a monthly advice column for* Parenting *magazine.*

At the dawn of your diapering career, you necessarily focus on learning how to do it right, so that the diaper stays on and in the correct position to work its high-absorbency magic. But like anything you practice at least ten times a day every day, soon enough you become a pro at the mechanics of diapering and can quite literally do it in your sleep. Then is the time to start thinking about what I like to call your diapering etiquette quotient (DEQ).

It is the rare parent who starts out with a high DEQ—it requires many a faux pas, raised eyebrow, and later reflection for most of us to get there. Although I am giving you advice today, I can recall a restaurant dinner with friends (childless at the time) during which I thought nothing of changing my baby's, shall we say, fragrant diaper in the booth right there at the table, just as the others were digging into their main course. Delicious. These nice friends said nothing, but their faces registered disgust, surprise, or maybe both. Lesson learned: no diaper changing at the dining table, whether in a restaurant or a home, whether you think the diaper contains number one or two. Excuse yourself and take your baby to the restroom or the backseat of your car, change her diaper, and get back to your dinner party. It is a small price to pay to avoid being called a, um, party pooper.

Must you always be so considerate? No—the more adult-oriented the situation (a restaurant, a dinner party, a movie theater, an art museum, the office), the more you should err on the side of being overly discreet about diaper changing. At more kid-oriented places (the playground, a children's museum, the mall, the beach), you can get away with a little less discretion, partly because of the blur of child activity swirling around you. When in doubt, you can always ask, "Hey, will it bother anybody if I change the baby's diaper over here?"

As for the specifics of good DEQ, they include small but important considerations, such as *always* placing a waterproof pad under your baby's bottom before diapering him on someone else's couch, bed, rug, or table, even if you are long past taking this precaution in your own home. Then make your changing routine swift and inconspicuous. Don't stop to have a conversation while your baby's privates are on display—they may be amazing or barely noticeable to you, but to the rest of us, they're best kept undercover, hence the term *private* parts. If you have a boy who may be a sprayer, lay the clean diaper over his penis immediately after opening the dirty diaper.

Other DEQ do's: Stick the dirty wipe in the dirty diaper, and use the diaper to wrap it all up neatly together. Keep a stash of plastic bags in your diaper bag to hold your used diapers (newspaper delivery bags and bread bags are good for this); then, whenever humanly possible, take these with you to dispose of in your own trash at home. When this is not possible (because you're traveling or just out for the day), ask your hosts where to dispose of this package. Do not, I repeat, do not just toss it in the powder room trash basket. Left to fester, this is about the nastiest hostess "gift" you can give, and believe me, you will be remembered for it.

Finally, after diapering your baby, *always* wash your hands thoroughly. Whether or not you are going back into the kitchen to cook, others will appreciate you for your sensitive and sanitary ways.

30

BE A STYLISH NEW MOM

LIZ LANGE

Liz Lange is president and founder of Liz Lange Maternity,
a line of clothing distributed through her stores across the
country. She designs a line of maternity clothing for Target
and is the author of Liz Lange's Maternity Style.

A s a new mom, fashion is probably one of the last things on your mind. Instead of being consumed with the latest Balenciaga bag, your thoughts are now focused on having the right bottle, diaper, crib, or stroller. At the same time, you will likely be itching to get back into your prepregnancy clothes. Sadly, almost no woman's body magically snaps back into perfect shape directly after having a baby. But as a new mom, you certainly don't have to look like a sweat-suit-swaddled mess. Rest assured: there are some simple and easy ways to look chic and pulled together. By sticking to some of my perennial, all body-type fashion guidelines, you'll be able to step out in style to show off your new bundle of joy.

FOURTH TRIMESTER

Postpregnancy maternity dressing is something all women with children know about, but few choose to talk about. Don't be embarrassed to return to wearing your first-trimester maternity favorites! I like to refer to the postpregnancy period as the "fourth trimester." Of course, the duration of the fourth trimester is based on the individual. It's been a few weeks for some women I know and for others it's been a year. Don't go out and buy a whole new fourth-trimester wardrobe of nonmaternity clothes. You will be able to wear them only on the way back down to your prepregnancy weight.

PRACTICAL MATERIALS

Stretch cotton should be your best friend as a new mom. It will fit you no matter what your body looks like. It's also reliable because you can wash it over and over after getting spit up on!

TUMMY SLIMMING STYLES

Draw attention away from your tummy by wearing fun and of-the-moment tunic tops. They hide flaws and are slimming and comfortable. Another flattering option is the A-line shift dress—it's great for dress-up occasions. Fitted jeans with a stretchy underbelly are a must-have for all new moms. Denim has become the ultimate go-to item for dressing up or dressing down.

STYLES TO AVOID

As in pregnancy dressing, abstain from wearing loose, shapeless clothes. They will only make you look bigger. Instead, opt for slim, sleek, and stretchy styles that are fitted but never tight.

SHOES

So many women's weakness and rightly so, shoes are the perfect way to complement a simple outfit or to show off your personality. As a new mom, you may not have as much occasion to wear the sky-high stilettos you once wore since you'll be running around so much. Again, this doesn't mean you have to forsake your sense of style. Add to your shoe wardrobe by investing in some stylish ballet flats, cool sneakers, or sweet kitten heels.

ACCESSORIES

I'm not a huge proponent of carrying a diaper bag. As a new mom, I used my favorite large pocketbook and put all my baby items in large ziplock bags which I shoved right in. I felt more like "me" not using a diaper bag, but if you choose to use one you'll certainly find a great selection of hip, cool ones on the market today. Jewelry that's classic and not too fussy is another way to spice up any look.

IN A PINCH

One of my absolute fashion mantras is to rely on the "dipped look." A monochromatic dressing scheme where you "dip" yourself in one color, whether black, charcoal gray, navy, camel, or even white, is the easiest and best way to look incredibly chic. Add a few colorful accessories and you're ready to go!

31

NURTURE YOUR MARRIAGE

Carol Ummel Lindquist

Dr. Carol Ummel Lindquist is a marriage counselor,

psychologist, and the author of Happily Married with Kids:

It's Not Just a Fairy Tale.

At first it may seem impossible to refocus on your relationship with your partner, but this is an essential part of raising a happy child. Happy couples raise socially, emotionally, and financially more successful children. What follows is a collection of tips to help you to maintain—and even improve—your life as a contented spouse and devoted parent.

It is fair to say that you can expect some major changes after the birth of your first child. Adaptability to change is the hallmark of a happy marriage and, in turn, a happy family. Instead of thinking of yourselves as a couple with problems, think of yourselves as a *problem-solving couple.* My husband insists that we never fight; instead, we clearly communicate. View your marriage as a partnership that you create together and have control over.

One of the most difficult challenges that new parents face is finding time alone together. While bonding with your newborn is one of the most important things you can do as a parent, spending time away is also essential. Establishing a regular and comfortable child-care routine early on will help your child's social ease and make it easier to plan future nights out. Many resourceful couples build their alone time into their daily routines. If you both work, clear your midday schedules and sneak out to lunch together. Make each other your priority after your child's bedtime.

Plan overnight getaways together. Take the nanny along, or leave your child with family or friends. When your child is very young, one night may be all you can manage, but as a child grows older, longer stays will be possible. Sometimes several families will travel together, allowing one couple to watch the kids while the others take a night out. Other parents create babysitting co-ops.

After the birth of a new baby, couples soon realize that the concept of time as they knew it has changed forever. Because your time is that much more precious, it is important to see time with your mate as two distinct types: romantic time and problem-solving time. Be mindful of keeping the two separate; otherwise, you will wind up fighting during dinner at an expensive restaurant over whose turn it is to do the laundry. Regularly ruining date nights may lead you both to avoid making them in the future, so relax and enjoy your time together, and save the problem solving for later. Please note that occasionally falling asleep during date night is completely normal.

"Romantic time" can take on many different forms. Most important, make time to focus on each other. Taking the time to hang out, have fun, and be affectionate is the key to maintaining a healthy and happy relationship.

Spend time with other happily married couples with children. Families with children will help you to see that your problems are completely normal. Other couples will probably have eccentric and creative ways to solve the challenges that lie ahead.

Be mindful that your spouse is also an individual. A wife who encourages her husband's golf outings or a husband who encourages a wife's night out with friends will strengthen their marriage and ensure that they can continue to grow closer as a couple.

Being creative in finding time together as a couple will not only help you to create the kind of marriage that you want but will also help create a happy family. Maintaining a happy marriage after children is not just a fairy tale!

32

MAINTAIN YOUR SEX LIFE

VALERIE DAVIS RASKIN

Dr. Valerie Davis Raskin is a psychiatrist in private practice in Chicago. She is past president of the Illinois Psychiatric Society and the author of three books, including Great Sex for Moms: Ten Steps to Nurturing Passion While Raising Kids.

$\mathbf{A}$ drop in your libido is perfectly normal after the birth of a baby. Many a new mother has recoiled in horror when her obstetrician tells her it's okay to resume lovemaking after the six-week postpartum checkup. At four months postpartum, 20 percent of couples have not resumed intercourse; at one year, 90 percent of couples are having sex but only about once a week.

Why bother if you never seem to want it? Here are some reasons to insist on great sex after baby:

It's good for you. Keeping a sexual groove going reminds you that you are more than an infant-care machine. Plus it's fun—even if you would never initiate sex, once you get going you'll rediscover that it isn't gum surgery.

It's good for your baby. If you believe that what your child needs is an exhausted but always self-sacrificing mom, you're ignoring the divorce statistics. Sex is a buffer during times of stress, and for many couples this is the hardest time in their marriage. Intimate couples are generally more resilient, nicer to each other, and more likely to give each other the benefit of the doubt when conflict flares. It's what makes marriage more than an economic or residential partnership, and why parental sex is a family value.

It's good for your partner. No, he isn't a self-centered chimpanzee because he wants sex more than you do, and he isn't lying when he says he doesn't notice the extra pounds. Sex is one of the only things he can give you that your baby can't, and he needs to know that he matters, too.

Maintaining a good sex life after the birth of a baby requires *intention, attention, communication,* and *mutual kindness.* Here are some tips:

You have to make time. Spontaneous sex is gone for now, and chances are late-night sex will always seem less attractive than late-night sleep. Have sex during the baby's morning nap. Ask Grandma or a babysitter to take the baby out for an afternoon stroll for an hour, turn off the phone, and *do it.* Trade a few hours of baby watching with a girlfriend, and plan to make love, ignoring the laundry.

You have to work with your body. Lube, lube, and more lube is often critical after childbirth. Your pharmacy sells Astroglide, which makes intercourse more comfortable and can increase the pleasure of touch when applied externally over the vulva and clitoris. Don't get stuck thinking sex equals intercourse, because "outercourse" (manual and/or oral sex) may be much more pleasurable in the first few months and a nice option for a "quickie."

Talk, show, and listen. One way to want more sex: make it better. You may have put up with so-so sex in the old days, but now it needs to be worth the time and effort. If you haven't usually climaxed in the past, here's your opportunity. Your sexual partner cannot read your mind, so you will need to teach him how best to please you. You can do this by guiding his touch to the right spot or right pressure, or tell him what feels best or what your fantasies are. Ask him to show you what he likes. Be brave.

Be kind. Whenever possible, use praise rather than criticism in the bedroom. "I love having your mouth on me" works better than "Why are you so hung up about oral sex?" Avoid scorn, labeling, and escalation. Assume that both of you are doing the best you can under the circumstances, and recognize that libido mismatches are a shared concern.

33

EMBRACE YOUR ROLE
AS A NEW MOTHER

ANN PLESHETTE MURPHY

Ann Pleshette Murphy is the author of The 7 Stages
of Motherhood: Loving Your Life Without Losing Your
Mind. *She is the parenting contributor for* Good Morning
America, *the ParentSmart columnist for* USA WEEKEND,
and was the editor in chief of Parents *magazine for ten years.*

$\mathbf{M}$ otherhood is a seismic transformation, and in order to embrace your new role you must let go of the expectation that you will simply pick up where you left off. Having a baby is more than a minor change. Your life will never be the same—but that's actually very good news, because in both mundane and monumental ways it will be so much better.

FORGET ABOUT "GETTING BACK TO NORMAL"
As understandable as it may be to expect to get back to your old routine in a couple of months, take the pressure off yourself during your first postpartum weeks: accept that there's nothing "normal" about days that merge into nights, a body that balloons

and sags in bizarre and sometimes painful ways, and a heart that pumps equal amounts of passion and panic. If you manage to feed and change your baby and take a short walk, pat yourself on the back. Every time you respond to your baby's cries or put on her onesie a little more efficiently or sync your nap with hers, you've *done* a lot, even if these minor acts of caring are difficult to articulate when your husband comes home and asks, "So what did you two do today?"

YOUR HUSBAND ISN'T YOU

This may seem obvious, but many new moms are shocked to discover that the man they love most in the world, the soul mate with whom they've always walked in matched steps, seems to be orbiting in a far-off galaxy. It's not just that he manages to sleep through nighttime howls that would rouse the dead or that he's not the diaper champ you envisioned. He may also be on a very different wavelength emotionally. When he fails to share your anxiety about finding the perfect babysitter, exhibits no guilt about leaving the baby with his mother so you two can go out together, or actually tries to convince you that six weeks is ample time to wait before resuming sex, remember that it takes a while to transition from partners to parents. Accept that his way may not be your way and tell him clearly but gently what's bothering you.

Most important, avoid what I call "the expert/dumb apprentice trap." Don't micromanage or jump in with "constructive criticism" (the ultimate oxymoron) when he puts Baby's T-shirt on backward. Unless he's doing something that's potentially life threatening, leave him alone with the baby and go take a walk.

GET THE HELP YOU NEED AND REJECT THE HELP YOU DON'T

Most moms have a major problem asking for help. We're made to believe that motherhood comes naturally and that asking for help is tantamount to admitting failure. Believe me, every mother on the planet needs help and support, but not all helpers are created equal. Your mother-in-law may be banging down doors to get her hands on her new grandchild, but if you're thinking of getting your hands around Grandma's neck within an hour of her arrival, then she's not a good choice. If the child-care provider you hire makes you feel like a bumbling rookie or is so obsequious that you know she would never, ever voice her opinion, then she's not the person to hire.

What you need more than anything is someone or a group of some-ones who are there for *you*. It takes enormous energy, compassion, patience, creativity, determination, and sacrifice to be a mother and none of us can go it alone. When you're feeling exhausted, angry, lonely, or all of the above, pick up the phone and ask questions or talk to others who can relate. Only by nurturing yourself can you fully embrace your new role as a mom.

34

TAKE CARE OF YOURSELF AS A NEW MOTHER

DEBRA GILBERT ROSENBERG

Debra Gilbert Rosenberg is a psychotherapist and the author of
The New Mom's Companion: Care for Yourself While You
Care for Your Newborn *and* Motherhood Without Guilt: Being
the Best Mother You Can Be and Feeling Great About It.

As a new mom, you are probably so busy taking care of others that you sometimes forget to take care of yourself. You may even believe that your own needs should be ignored while you put all your efforts into keeping the rest of the family happy and comfortable. You may worry or feel guilty that if you indulge yourself even a little, you won't be as good a mother. But if you *don't* make sure that you, too, are well rested, well fed, and have an adequate amount of time to socialize, relax, and maintain your most important relationships, you won't have the emotional or physical energy to care for your family. Instead, see this as an opportunity to teach your kids that it's possible to be a well-rounded person who can take care of others while also leading a full and enjoyable life. Taking care of yourself while you care for your newborn is neither unimportant nor selfish; it allows you to be a happier and more efficient mother, worker, friend, daughter, and life partner.

Treat yourself as you would a treasured employee. Reassess your priorities and be thoughtful about what needs to get accomplished. Here are some suggestions:

* Make sure that every day you take some time—even if it's only 20 minutes—to do something you personally enjoy, alone or with your kids, your friends, or your mate.
* Eat a well-balanced meal and get enough rest every day.
* Remember that sharing the highlights of your day with your mate and playing with your children are every bit as important as scrubbing the toilets.
* Reconsider your standards; remind yourself that as long as you are all alive and content at the end of each day, you've done a good job. Your children want to spend time with you; if there is edible food and the house is clean enough to be safe, they won't care if you vacuum daily, weekly, or monthly.
* Reevaluate what's important to you. When it's a beautiful night take everyone outside and stargaze; skipping the occasional bath is just fine.
* Eliminate (or seriously limit) unnecessary contact with people or tasks you dislike.
* Remember that good mothers are not necessarily good cooks or housekeepers. If you weren't good at something before you became a mother, you won't suddenly become Susie Homemaker now. And that is just fine.

* Lower your standards just a bit. Maybe you can shower (or bathe the baby, make the bed, etc.) only once every 36 or 48 hours, and still be presentable. Some tasks just don't need to be done quite so often, and doing some things less often frees you up for more fun.
* Be flexible; make changes in your life when you feel your choices aren't working for you.

You will be more effective in all aspects of motherhood if you take care of your own emotional and personal needs. Just remember to include yourself on your list of important things to nurture, because when Mom is happy, everybody else is happy, too.

35

BE A GREAT FATHER

Armin Brott

*Armin Brott, known as Mr. Dad, writes the nationally
syndicated column "Ask Mr. Dad" and hosts the syndicated radio
show* Positive Parenting. *He is the author of* The Expectant
Father *and* The New Father: A Dad's Guide to the First Year.

The secret to being a great dad is to get involved as early as possible—preferably before the baby even arrives—and then stay involved.

1. BE A REAL PARTICIPANT. Go to all of your partner's OB visits, hear your baby's heartbeat, and watch him squirm around in the ultrasound. Take a childbirth prep course and commit to being with your partner throughout the whole labor and delivery.

2. GET THINGS SETTLED AT WORK. Very few companies offer paid leave for dads, but check with your Human Resources Department to see whether you're eligible for some unpaid time off under the Family Leave Act. If not, save up as much vacation and sick time as you can. Either way, prepare

your employer and your co-workers for your absence as far in advance as possible. The more notice you give them, the more supportive they'll be.

3. JUMP IN! Don't assume that your partner is magically better at parenting than you are. Whatever she knows, she learned on the job—and by making a lot of mistakes. And the way you're going to get better is by making your own mistakes. Trust your instincts first. Chances are you'll do exactly the right thing. If you do need help, ask for it.

4. DON'T WASTE A SECOND. The sooner you start holding and caring for your baby, the sooner you'll learn what he needs and what you have to do to comfort him. In the first year, your baby mostly needs to feel safe and loved. So cuddle, talk, sing, read, dance, and show him the sights, sounds, and smells of his new world.

5. BE A PARTNER NOT JUST A HELPER. After money, couples argue most about who does what around the house. The more responsibility you take on, the happier your partner will be, the happier you'll be, and the stronger your relationship will be.

6. TAKE CHARGE. Unless you take the initiative, you'll never be able to be the father you want to be and the one your children need you to be. So instead of letting your partner pluck a crying or smelly baby from your arms, try something like, "No, honey, I can take care of this," or "That's okay—I really need the practice." There's nothing wrong with asking her for advice. But have her tell you how instead of doing it for you.

7. STAND YOUR GROUND. If you're feeling left out, or if your partner seems reluctant to share the parenting with you, talk to her about

it. But be gentle. Many women have been raised to believe that if they aren't the primary caregivers (even if they work outside the home as well), they've somehow failed as mothers. Show her that you're serious about wanting to be an equal participant and that you're ready and able to do the job.

8. SUPPORT BREASTFEEDING. Ideally, your baby should have nothing but breast milk for the first six months. But nursing is sometimes hard for new moms. Make sure your partner gets plenty of fluids and rest, and tell her often what a great job she's doing. The more encouraging you are, the longer she's likely to breastfeed and the more she'll enjoy it.

9. DON'T FORGET YOUR RELATIONSHIP. Before you became parents, you and your partner spent a lot of time together, building your relationship. But now your baby is the focus of nearly everything you do. You barely have time to sleep, let alone do the things that brought you together in the first place. Set aside some time every day to talk about something other than the baby. It's harder than it sounds but well worth the effort.

36

DEVELOP GOOD PARENTING HABITS

LAURENCE STEINBERG

Dr. Laurence Steinberg is the Distinguished University
Professor of Psychology at Temple University. He is the
author of numerous books, including The 10 Basic
Principles of Good Parenting.

Good parenting is a lot more scientific than most people think. After decades of research, we know what works, and we know why. That's great news, because it means that *anyone* can learn to be a good parent. Even better, the same basic principles of good parenting work regardless of your child's sex, age, birth order, or your family's background.

Here are ten things every parent should know:

1. TAILOR YOUR PARENTING TO YOUR CHILD'S STAGE OF DEVEL-OPMENT. Learn about each stage of development that your child goes through before he or she gets there. The more you understand about child development, the easier it is to be a

good parent. Make sure your knowledge keeps pace with your child.

2. BE A MINDFUL PARENT. How you treat and respond to your child should come from an informed, deliberate sense of what you want to accomplish. Think about what you do before you do it.

3. BE CONSISTENT. Children thrive on predictability and routine. Don't change your parenting from day to day. Work out your differences with your partner so that you are both on the same page about how you will respond to various disciplinary challenges. Have a regular schedule for bedtime, naps, and meals.

4. DON'T HOLD BACK ON EXPRESSIONS OF AFFECTION. You can spoil a child rotten with material possessions, but not with genuine love. The warmer you are toward your child, the better off she will be.

5. NEVER SPANK OR HIT YOUR CHILD. Physical punishment is harmful and dangerous, and it's an ineffective form of discipline. Never means never.

6. DON'T FIGHT YOUR CHILD'S DISPOSITION. A fearful child can't help being fearful, nor can an active child help being active. You can't refashion your child's disposition. Learn to adapt to your baby's temperament, rather than forcing your baby to adapt to you.

7. LET YOUR CHILD DEVELOP AT HIS OWN SPEED. Your baby will wean himself, learn how to use a spoon, walk, and talk just fine without you trying to move things along on what you think the "right" schedule is. Childhood is not a race to see who gets to the next stage first. If you are worried that your child is developing too slowly, check with your pediatrician.

8. DON'T TURN EVERY INTERACTION WITH YOUR CHILD INTO A "LEARNING EXPERIENCE." Your child will benefit more from rolling around on the floor with you than from a session with flash cards. Get in the habit of just having fun time together.

9. EXPOSE YOUR CHILD TO LANGUAGE. Probably the biggest contributor to babies' cognitive development and later success in school is their exposure to language. Talk to your child, even if she's not talking yet. Point out things that she seems to be noticing ("Do you see the doggie?") and explain what you are doing while you are doing it ("Now I'm going to wash your feet."). From the start, read to your child on a daily basis.

10. PARENTING IS NOT A PART-TIME ENDEAVOR. Parenting is not something you do just when you feel like it or only when your child is in some sort of need. Your baby is going to grow up faster than you can possibly imagine, and when your child is about to leave home as a young adult you won't be saying to yourself, "I wish I had spent less time with my child." If you have the right attitude and are determined to keep learning, there's nothing more fun or rewarding than being a parent.

37

TRUST YOUR INSTINCTS AS A NEW PARENT

Lu Hanessian

Lu Hanessian is the author of Let the Baby Drive: Navigating the Road of New Motherhood. *She is the host of* Make Room for Baby *on Discovery Health Channel and a contributing writer to* Fit Pregnancy. *Her CD of original ballads is called* Welcome Home, My Child: Songs for a Mother's Journey.

Parenting without intuition is like flying without radar. Although you've read every how-to, where-to, and when-to prior to delivery, once you meet your baby, you realize that there is, in fact, no universal baby playbook. Your newborn blinks at you as if to say, "Work with me. . . ." But how do you hear, let alone trust, your own voice—and your baby's—amid the roar of the crowd?

Let go of expectations. Most of us cross the frontier of parenthood harboring fantasies of what we expected when we were expecting. Inevitably, our expectations and our experience collide somewhere in the *fourth* trimester. Holding on to expectations after the birth tends to drain your energy, breed disappointment, cloud your thinking, and keep your intuitive self at bay. Trusting your intuition as a parent allows you to invest in the present moment, and be flexible enough to change with the circumstances. Stop mulling over what has already happened or worrying about what has yet to unfold. When you stay focused on the here and now, you can tune into details you may have otherwise missed.

Get adequate rest. Sleep deprivation, while inevitable in new parenthood, can distort the senses. In the newborn months, sleep when your baby sleeps. Sleep *for* your baby. As he grows, seize every opportunity to rest and recharge physically and mentally. Learn to power nap. Pare down your "To Do" list. It's very hard to trust yourself in the fog of exhaustion.

Don't take everyone's word for it. As a new parent, you will invariably hear voices. Relatives, friends, even strangers, might feel compelled to share their well-meaning advice. Some may question your parenting style. Others may feel inclined to warn you that your choices will backfire. It can be helpful to rely on others for information, reassurance, perspective, and even hope if you need it, but trust your ability to sort through the multitude of opinions to identify what is right for your family.

Trust your baby. If at first you don't trust your own instincts, trust your child's. Think small. When in doubt, ask yourself what you would want if you were in your baby's booties. Babies know what they need. Their cry is their language. What is your baby telling you? What is your response? A baby's innocence should not be mistaken for ignorance. His needs must never be mistaken for manipulations. Babies have no ulterior motives. When you trust your baby, you are teaching him to trust himself.

Acknowledge your fears. You worry that you are "doing it wrong," that the baby's needs will consume you, that you can never keep your child safe in an uncertain world, that you feel as helpless as your newborn. Instead of letting your fear determine your choices, trust yourself to figure out what's driving that fear—before it drives you to parent defensively. Chronic stress doesn't just affect your physical and emotional well-being; it affects a baby's mind, body, and spirit as well.

Trusting yourself as a parent is not about being right all the time, but rather about knowing when to confer with others for insight and when to rely on your hunch that something's amiss even when people tell you otherwise. And if in doubt, dive into your own research and investigate a situation thoroughly. When you trust your intuition, self-doubt becomes a compass, not a reason to second-guess yourself. Ultimately, the practice of tuning into your baby's intuitive needs— and your own—will guide you to doing "right" by your child and yourself.

38

HANDLE UNSOLICITED PARENTING ADVICE

PAULA SPENCER

Paula Spencer is the author of Momfidence! An Oreo Never
Killed Anybody and Other Secrets of Happier Parenting.
She writes the "Momfidence" column in Woman's Day *magazine.*
She's also a longtime contributing editor of Parenting *and*
Babytalk *magazines. Her first book was* Everything ELSE You
Need to Know When You're Expecting: The New Etiquette
for the New Mom.

"He needs a hat."
"I know just the thing to cure that thumb-sucking . . ."
"She'll never get to Harvard if you don't . . ."

Everybody has an opinion about how to raise a baby. What's a
nice mom (or dad) supposed to do—especially when you've
heard enough? Fortunately, there are happier options than
grousing "Mindyourownbusiness!" or bursting into tears:

1. CONSIDER THE MOTIVATION. Most critics don't even think of themselves as being critical. They consider their meddling as "involved," "loving," and "caring." It doesn't feel very warm and fuzzy to be told by an anonymous four-foot-tall babushka that wearing your baby in a sling will make your little tyke bowlegged, but most unsolicited parenting advice springs from good intentions, if bad manners. Clucking and sharing lets veteran moms participate vicariously in your baby days. They're just trying, in their own boundary-crashing way, to help.

2. TAKE NOTHING PERSONALLY. Think of advice as a benign, neutral substance. Like wine, it's how we interact with it that makes life better, or worse. Take a few sips and you smile. Wallow in the stuff and you fall on the floor.

    Parenting advice plays to the heart of our anxiety. We all want to be the best parents we can be. So we tend to hear any input that's counter to what we're doing already as proof-positive that we're screwing up. But we're not! There are as many "right" ways to parent as there are busybodies with opinions about the subject. Drink up advice cheerfully and in moderation, or politely ignore it. Just don't let it get to you.

3. SKIM THE CREAM; TOSS THE REST. Just because you didn't ask for the tip doesn't mean it's worthless. Stay open-minded. I once learned a better burping hold from a friend whose ideas on infant care previously had me wheeling my Bugaboo in the opposite direction when I saw her. And I might still be struggling to keep the kids' tennis shoes tied if a perfect stranger on a playground hadn't volunteered the virtues of Velcro.

4. PERFECT THE DEFLECT. Two little phrases to master: "Really?" and "Hmmm . . . I'll have to look into that." Sound vaguely interested—but only enough to be polite. Come across too fascinated, and you'll egg the advicemonger on.

   Whatever you do, don't argue—even if the advice is wacky or plain wrong. It just drags the lecture out. And do be nice, especially when elders are involved. Nobody likes to hear her advice is thirty years behind the times—even if it is.

5. BLAME THE DOCTOR. When my firstborn had colic, my mother-in-law was sure he was starving ("Or maybe it's a tapeworm!"). My mom was pushing a baby cereal invented during the Depression. My pediatrician just chuckled, not at the colic but at me. "Don't you know, no grandmother's baby ever cried?" he said. He told me to tell them that he—the Mighty Doctor—had said I was handling my colicky son just right. It worked! They backed off. I've used the doctor tactic to ward off critics countless times since then (on picky eaters, discipline, toilet training . . .). Especially when the advice sounds complicated, cruel, or questionable, just say, "Thanks. I'll be sure to ask Dr. X."

6. KNOW WHEN TO MAKE A CHANGE. When all else fails, switch the subject. Ask your lecturer's opinion about some inane topic you don't really care about, like their recommended color for a blankie. But if they go on and on—or go back to grinding their original ax—resort to the handy exit line that is the prerogative of every new parent: "Excuse us; it's time for a diaper change."

39

FIND YOUR INNER PATIENCE

JAN FAULL

Jan Faull has been a parent educator for more than twenty-five

years and is the author of four books, including

Darn Good Advice—Baby. *Her weekly parenting*

column appears in the Seattle Times.

P arents of newborns need copious amounts of patience as their infant adjusts to the world. Before birth, all of your baby's needs were perfectly attended to, but now he seeks you out to provide food, interaction, security, and comfort. He can't survive without you. At first, deciphering your baby's cries, expressions, and movements is a guessing game, but soon you'll know just how to respond. A patient approach will guide you.

When you're rushing out the door to a doctor appointment and your infant poops into his cute little outfit, take a deep breath, head back to the nursery, and, like a quick-change artist, clean and dress your baby again. Don't hurry through the process or your baby will sense your tenseness and respond with distressful cries. You'll be fifteen minutes late, so be it.

No doubt when you're rested and well fed, patience comes more easily. That's why it's important to have at least one adult who will look after you during the first month of your baby's life. That person could be your spouse, partner, mother, grandmother, sister, neighbor, or friend. This person will bring you food, hold the baby while you sleep, and offer a helping hand with dishes, laundry, and grocery shopping.

Being rushed contributes to impatience. Most parents today are constantly on the go with schedules to meet, and activities and work to keep up with. You'll do best by your baby and yourself if you slow your life down. You may need to temporarily replace going to the movies, unnecessary shopping, and hiking in the woods with renting DVDs, shopping online, and strolling with your baby around the block. Allow yourself many mornings, afternoons, and evenings with no planned agenda except time for you and your baby. If you're stressed, your baby will be also.

You'll also develop patience more easily if you're well informed. Read about babies' sleeping, eating, and growing patterns. If you have realistic expectations, you won't pressure your child to behave or learn beyond what's reasonable for his developmental age.

Being a patient parent, however, doesn't mean being overindulgent. When your baby becomes a toddler, he might resist getting into his car seat. Wait him out. Distract him by singing a song. It might take a couple of minutes—patience is the key.

Another avenue for developing patience is to join a parent support group where you can share the joys and frustrations of parenting. All the better if there's a pediatric nurse or parent educator to lead the group and offer sound advice. Instead of a gripe session, your support group can serve as an exchange of information to give you the strength and resources to be the patient parent you want to be.

When you sense that you're about to lose your patience, breathe deeply until the tense moment passes. Ask yourself, "What does my child need? What do I need? How can we move through this situation with patience, grace, and dignity?" If you find yourself losing your patience over and over, it might be time to talk to a professional, someone who understands children and will offer you options to remedy the situation.

All children deserve your patience as they learn, develop, and work toward growing in the time frame that is uniquely theirs.

40

MANAGE RELATIONSHIPS WITH YOUR PARENTS AND IN-LAWS

GAIL SALTZ

Dr. Gail Saltz is a clinical associate professor of psychiatry at the New York–Presbyterian Hospital Weill-Cornell School of Medicine. She is a psychoanalyst with the New York Psychoanalytic Institute and has a private practice in Manhattan. Saltz is the mental health contributor on NBC's Today. *She writes a weekly relationship column on MSNBC.com and is the author of three books, including* Anatomy of a Secret Life: The Psychology of Living a Lie.

What do you do when your mother wants to run the show or when your mother-in-law acts angry and hurt if she is not included? What about the grandparent who just isn't that interested?

The relationship between parent and grandparent can be complicated. Most women find that pregnancy and early parenting revive many of the conflicts they felt as a child with their own mothers. You may spend a lot of time thinking about your own childhood, and the intensity of feelings both positive and negative for your mother and father may return. While this is all very normal, it can make for greater closeness and also greater conflict.

Exploring your own feelings about your parents can be useful in sorting out how you yourself want to parent. However, it's also important to understand that your parents have dedicated a very large portion of their lives (and a lot of their emotional energy) to parenting. They probably believe that their primary identity is that of a parent—a very good parent who gave great thought to raising you (or your spouse) and worrying about your happiness and well-being. They want to feel that you, too, believe they did an excellent job of child rearing. Consequently, they may feel that anything you and your spouse do differently with your children than they did with you is like a declaration of disapproval. For instance, when you decide to wean your child from breast straight to a cup (even though you were bottle-fed) or go back to work when your mother stayed home, realize that she may take this as a criticism of her parenting decisions.

WHAT TO DO

Try to preemptively talk to your parents and your in-laws. Tell them you appreciated your upbringing and that while you admire what they did as parents, you and your spouse want to make your own choices. Negotiate all major child-rearing decisions with your spouse only. Similarly, avoid confiding to your parents any big disagreements you and your partner have over child rearing. On the other hand, be sure to invite your parents to participate in the fun and meaningful moments you have with their new grandchild and show them that you really value their presence.

Give your parents and in-laws time alone with the grandkids. This can give you a much-needed break for romantic time while also allowing them to develop their own relationship with your child. It also lets the grandparents know that you trust them with the kids. If grandparents are older and too much alone time with Baby is wearing, even brief periods are good.

On the opposite end of the spectrum from the overly involved grandparent, the uninterested grandparent may not be great with small children. Becoming a grandparent may make him or her feel old, and your child may be a reminder of that. Plan "youthful" activities that make it easier for both grandparents and child to feel active without requiring the reluctant grandparents to invent activities. Go to the circus, plan a baking project, or spend a day at the beach. Once your parents use these times to get to know your child, they may find it easier to play together later. Don't force it if your parents don't feel comfortable with playing—this will just create frustration for all of you.

Remember: your parents and in-laws are older and interested in their next stage of life, which means enjoying some freedom. Envying that freedom, because you have just given up your own, can also lead to conflicts. Expect that there might be times when you want them to help you out but they are busy. Being sensitive to and validating their feelings, and sharing smaller issues of child rearing yet being firm in making larger decisions with only your spouse, will go a long way in making your new grandparent relationship a mutually satisfying one.

41

BE A LOVING GRANDPARENT

ARTHUR KORNHABER

Dr. Arthur Kornhaber is a child and family psychiatrist and

the author of eight books, including his most recent,

The Grandparent Solution: How Parents Can Build a Family

Team for Practical, Emotional, and Financial Success.

He is the president and founder of the nonprofit Foundation

for Grandparenting, and Tom Brokaw called him

"the Dr. Spock of Grandparenting."

J ean-Paul Sartre, the French writer and philosopher, said that he could make his grandmother go into raptures of joy just by being hungry.

This simple memory reveals a great deal about the special nature of the grandparent-grandchild bond, a relationship completely different from that of parents and children. Time spent together, and one-to-one attention enhances this vital connection.

Children see the stardust in their grandparent's adoring eyes, and this love transports them to a place where they acquire emotional strength and connectedness, a feeling of security and belonging, and unique knowledge and experience they learn nowhere else.

The magical grandparent-child connection starts even before birth. While parents dream of their parenthood, future grandparents hope and dream about their future grandparenthood. There is a "drive to grandparent" in many people, a natural biological urge that is manifested by the millions of potential grandparents who are presently urging their children to have children. Grandparenthood offers an emotional and spiritual blueprint that gives meaning and usefulness to later life. All family members, and especially children, benefit from such gifts. Savvy parents know this and make sure to garden the relationship between their parents and their children.

Just as it has programmed people to be parents, nature has programmed many of us to be grandparents, and designed many roles to fulfill that function: living ancestor, family historian, mentor, spiritual guide, teacher, crony, and more. Once your grandchild is born, realize that your behavior in each of these roles offers a template for your grandchild to use as an example for his own grandparenthood one day.

Here are some tips for how to make your grandparenting a success:

1. Cultivate your relationship with a future in-law before your child gets married.
2. Always support the marriage.
3. Get involved in the planning for your new grandchild. Get a list of baby needs from your child and ask what you can supply.
4. Attend a birth education class with the new parents-to-be to get up to speed on modern birthing.
5. Ask the parents how you can help (with time or money) when the new baby arrives.

6. Be there when your grandchild is born.
7. Let the parents know that you are a resource for them and have an occasional "state of the family" meeting to assess how things are going and how you can help to the max.
8. Be an example of open, honest, and frank communication.
9. Be involved in your grandchild's life directly. Offer to go to school, doctor's visits, and so on, and be there for important occasions.
10. Be available to give the parents a respite by babysitting and taking the grandchild for a weekend.
11. If your grandchild can't come to you, go to her.

Parents play a role, too. They need to respect the needs of grandparents to bond with the child and to ask grandparents to help in any way they can whether it is with time, attention, or finances. Parents would do well to "think grandparent" before asking others to help with the child. Moreover, be sure to ask grandparents directly for their assistance rather than anticipating their responses. Parents must remember that becoming a grandparent is a transformative experience. That is why so many parents say, most often with a broad smile, that they wish their own parents treated them as well as they treat their grandchildren.

42

BATHE YOUR BABY

LILLIAN M. BEARD

Dr. Lillian M. Beard is a pediatrician in Silver Spring,
Maryland, and an associate clinical professor of pediatrics at the
George Washington University School of Medicine and Health
Sciences. She was named one of America's Top Doctors 2005 by
Consumers' Research Council of America and is the author of Salt
in Your Sock and Other Tried-and-True Home Remedies.

The first time you bathe your baby at home, you may feel like you are all thumbs. Have no fear. With a plan, bath time can be calming for you and your baby. Consider what's needed to achieve your goal of a clean and comfortable baby, and with a bit of practice, you will get there. Time and preparation are essential. During your baby's first weeks, until the umbilical cord stump drops off, sponge baths are recommended. Despite what this term suggests, clean, soft washcloths, or cotton balls, *not sponges,* are used.

SPONGE BATH ESSENTIALS
Setting: *Room temperature; about 78 degrees.*
Tools: *A flat surface, 3 large towels, 2 bowls of warm water, 3 washcloths, mild unscented soap, baby shampoo, dry baby clothes.*

STEPS FOR THE SPONGE BATH

* Place Baby, naked, on one towel on a flat surface; cover the lower half of his body with the second towel while bathing the upper part; then reverse, covering the opposite half.
* With a clean, unsoaped washcloth, dampened in one of the bowls of warm water, wash Baby's entire face; gently wipe the eyes starting from the inside corner by the nose and working outward. Wash Baby's hair by using a very wet washcloth or a cupped hand of water to wet Baby's head. Then with a tiny dab of shampoo, massage the head gently with your hand. Rinse well with a dampened washcloth.
* Swish mild soap in the second bowl creating warm, sudsy water. With the second washcloth, wash Baby's neck, outer ears, chest, abdomen (avoid wetting the area around the umbilical cord), hips, legs, feet, groin, and buttocks including all folds and creases. In the groin/buttocks area, for girls, wash from front to back. For boys, wash the area around the penis. Rinse each area with the unsoaped washcloth and pat dry.
* Wrap Baby in the third towel while gently drying his entire body including all creases. Dress Baby in dry clothes.

Once the umbilical cord completely separates and falls off, Baby is ready for a real bath. Daily baths are not necessary. However, a bath every few days will keep Baby smelling sweet. Again, the setting should be a warm, comfortable room. Wear clothing that can get wet, remove any scratchy jewelry, and allow some unhurried time for this pleasant ritual for you and Baby.

STEPS FOR THE REAL BATH

* At this point, you can substitute a bathinette (a baby bath incorporated into a changing table), baby tub, basin, or sink for those 2

bowls of warm water. Aside from the 2 bowls, assemble the same list of tools as were used for the sponge bath.

* Position the bathinette or basin at a height that allows you to comfortably handle and bathe Baby without having to bend over.
* With a large bath towel on the bottom surface, run 2–3 inches of water into the baby tub. Test the water's temperature with your elbow to ensure that it's comfortably warm. Note: because our hands are often in warm to hot water (with handwashing and dishwashing), the hand is less sensitive than an elbow to subtle water temperature differences.
* Completely undress Baby and gradually ease him into the bath while engaging him with your soothing baby talk. Hold him securely, with your arm under his opposite armpit and his back, head, neck, and shoulders resting on your forearm, as the palm of that hand secures his chest. This frees your other hand to wash his head, hair, and body and to reach for towels or other items. *Never leave Baby unattended in water.*
* During the bath, always anticipate Baby's sudden random movements such as a "startle" reflex or a change in posture or position. Hold tightly. Wet babies are slippery!
* Following the bath, Baby might enjoy the sensual pleasure of your gently massaging an unscented mild cream on his extremities, chest, tummy, then back and buttocks. Avoid using creams or lotions on Baby's face and neck.

Bath time is that special opportunity for moms and dads to individually spend quality time with Baby. After the bath, a snuggly feeding followed by quiet time generally ensures a restful sleep.

43

MASSAGE YOUR BABY

MICHELLE EBBIN

Michelle Ebbin is a massage therapist and the founder of Basic Knead. She is the author of Hands on Baby: A Guide to Baby Massage. *She created the Gaiam/Living Arts' Massage Practice video/DVD series as well as the original Reflexology Sox™, The Massage Shirt™, and the Baby Massage Shirt™.*

Massage is one of the most effective ways to soothe and communicate with your new baby. By combining touch, intimacy, play, and caregiving, it provides tremendous physical and psychological benefits for both baby and parent. Massage can help your baby sleep better, reduce fussiness, relieve gas and constipation, and even reduce colic. Baby massage is simple, safe, rewarding and, best of all, anyone can do it!

Before you begin to massage your baby, consult your pediatrician to get approval. Most babies can be massaged from the day they are born. For the first six months, babies will benefit greatly from a daily massage five to twenty minutes long. The best time for massage is when the baby is in a quiet, alert state. I recommend massaging after a bath, before bedtime. Always wait at least forty-five minutes after a feeding before massaging. Avoid massage if your baby has any kind of illness or skin rash/infection. It's best to wait at least one week after an immunization before massaging your baby. After that, avoid massaging directly on the injection area, which may still be sensitive.

To get started, you'll need a soft comforter, extra towels, and unscented, all-natural oil, such as grapeseed, or lotion. I don't recommend using commercial oils that may have a petroleum base. Make sure the room is warm, and consider playing some soothing music. Wash your hands, remove jewelry, and make sure your fingernails are not too sharp.

There are three basic positions for baby massage. Choose the most comfortable one for you.

1. Sit cross-legged on the floor or on a bed. With a comforter and towel placed in front of you, lay your baby on his or her back facing you, about an arm's length away.
2. Sit on a couch with a towel placed over your legs. Keep your legs parallel and close together. Lay your baby on his or her back facing you, resting on your legs.
3. If you prefer to stand, place your baby on the changing table, and stand in front of him/her so that your baby is facing you.

Warm some oil or lotion in your hands, place them on Baby's legs and look into his or her eyes. Ask permission to massage and if your baby gives any cues of resistance, you may want to wait until Baby is more receptive. If not, begin by massaging Baby's feet with your thumbs.

Feet and Legs: The feet and legs are the least vulnerable parts of the baby's body and the areas where Baby is most receptive to massage. After massaging both feet with your thumbs, move your hands to one leg and stroke gently from the ankle to the top of the leg and down. Always keep your hands soft and the pressure light. Massage the other leg as well.

Tummy and Chest: Place your hands on Baby's belly and stroke hand over hand in a circle around the belly button, always moving in a *clockwise* direction. Place your palms facedown, fingers pointing inward, and stroke down from just below the rib cage to the pelvis with one hand and then the other. Repeat each stroke several times. Next, place your hands on Baby's chest and trace a heart shape with your palms moving up to the shoulders and back down to the center of the chest.

Arms: Stroke each arm from wrist to shoulder, and back down. Massage Baby's hands with your thumbs.

Face: Massage Baby's cheeks and forehead with your thumbs.

Back: Turn Baby onto his/her tummy, horizontally in relation to you. Stroke from Baby's neck to the butt, alternating hands. Stroke from Baby's side to other side, alternating hands. This may put your baby to sleep!

44

GROOM YOUR BABY: TRIMMING NAILS, CUTTING HAIR, AND CLEANING EARS

CLAIRE MCCARTHY

Dr. Claire McCarthy is an instructor in pediatrics at Harvard

Medical School, an attending physician at Children's Hospital of

Boston, and co-director of the Pediatrics Department at Martha

Eliot Health Center, a neighborhood health service of Children's

Hospital. She is the author of two books, including Everyone's

Children, *is a senior medical editor for Harvard Health*

Publications, and a contributing editor for Parenting *magazine.*

I f only keeping Baby neat and clean were simply a matter of soap and water. But no, at some point nails and hair need trimming, and something needs to be done about that earwax buildup. Parents often dread these endeavors, because they are worried about hurting their baby in the process. But with a few tips (and some confidence!) these, too, can be tackled.

NAILS

Let's get cutting nails out of the way because it's likely the thing you will need to do first (babies are often born with nails long enough to scratch their faces), and it is also the scariest. I called on my spouse for help after my initial nail-cutting attempt with my first child drew blood. Five more children and about two decades of being a pediatrician later, I'm no longer afraid of it, having learned a few tricks:

* *Actual cutting isn't always necessary.* Sometimes the nails aren't so much long as sharp, and an emery board can take care of the problem nicely—and safely.
* *Use nail clippers designed for babies.* Clippers designed for grown-ups are much harder to manage (and look big enough for amputations when they get near a baby finger or toe).
* *Try doing it backward.* Even with the baby nail clippers you can't always see where the bottom edge is grabbing when you clip with the nail facing you. But if you turn the finger or toe around so the pad is facing you, and then use the thumb of the hand that isn't holding the clipper to pull the pad down slightly, you can see exactly where you are cutting—and avoid cutting skin.
* *Nibbling is a viable alternative.* All you nail-biters out there, your skills can be put to good use—and no metal need come near your baby.
* *Distraction helps.* My husband puts a favorite show or video on the television, sits our long-nailed kid in his lap with an open magazine or book to catch the nail clippings, and clips away. Then our child doesn't fight him, which makes the job much easier.

HAIR

We've all been there: your child's bangs are so long she bears a striking resemblance to Cousin It, or those long locks make everyone think your baby boy is a baby girl. A few quick snips of the scissors, you think, could fix it.

The good news is that unlike with nail cutting, there are people who do this stuff for parents all the time—and if it's more than a few snips, going to a hairdresser can be a good idea. Ask friends where they take their kids; ideally, you want to find someone who is good with children and reasonably priced. But for just a few snips, or if you are steady-handed enough to cut more, you can absolutely do it at home.

For best results, wet the hair first. To cut straight and quickly, you'll need sharp scissors (sewing scissors work well). The real trick is to keep the kid from moving. Here are a few tips:

* If your baby is really little and you can manage it, snip while he sleeps.
* Try singing a song with your child while you cut her hair.
* Have a helper dance around and be silly for distraction.
* If all else fails, have a helper hold the child's head. The downside of this is that kids don't like it, and screaming may ensue.
* Hold the hair in sections away from the head—that way, a sudden swivel is less likely to cause bloodshed.
* If things start going south, do it in two sittings. Better half-done bangs for a few hours than zigzag ones.

EARS

Cleaning them is easy—and you can definitely do it yourself. All you need to remember is this: *don't put anything inside the ear.* In my practice I've retrieved cotton out of ears and have seen scratched canals and perforated eardrums—all as a result of ear-cleaning attempts. Contrary to popular opinion, earwax is a good thing; it traps dust and other debris that gets into the ear, and then tiny hairs in the canal move it out. All you need to do is wipe the outside—preferably with a damp washcloth rather than a cotton swab, so you won't be tempted to go inside—and you're all set.

45

DRESS YOUR BABY

LUCY SYKES AND EUAN RELLIE

Lucy Sykes is the founder and designer of Lucy Sykes Baby, a
line of clothing for children from three months to eight years old.
Her husband, Euan Rellie, is the chairman of the company.

Just like the rest of us, babies can be dressed up or dressed
down, but they really like to be dressed comfortably. When we
first became parents, we had no idea what clothes our baby
should wear. The nurses at the hospital gave us a good piece of
advice: if it's a hot day and you would wear a T-shirt, then your
baby can, too. Basically, your baby doesn't need more clothing
than you do. With that said, let's get started.

First, if someone offers to throw you a baby shower, then
don't spend lots of money on your unborn tot—let the people
who love you do so instead. We were given some beautiful things
by friends and family: warm sweaters, little moccasin booties,
and cool striped scarves. Yet even with the generosity of friends
and family, you will need to do a bit of supplementing and you
will inevitably want to buy your baby clothing that meets your
specific tastes and needs.

THE LAYETTE

A layette is an assortment of all of the essential clothing your newborn will need upon arrival. You should purchase a layette in advance and include at least 6 onesies (simple, cotton one-piece bodysuits with snap and pop fasteners), 6 side snap T-shirts, 6 receiving blankets, 6 pairs of socks (Baby will likely kick these off, but you will keep trying), 3 lightweight nightgowns, 5 tops with pants or one piece outfits, 2 hats (the hospital will likely give you one), and 1 bunting or snowsuit if you live in a cold climate. It may sound like a lot, but babies need to change clothes an insane number of times; sometimes it feels as if they change every 15 minutes. Plan to keep a big laundry basket nearby at all times.

Here's what to consider when buying baby clothes:

* Look for pieces that allow easy diaper changing access.
* Layering works well in winter. Snug clothes look and feel good on babies. Two onesies and 2 romper suits in the winter will keep your little one pretty cozy.
* Do not spend more than you can afford, but do splurge occasionally.
* U.S. brands tend to be sized bigger than international brands.
* As for colors, we recommend clean white for most clothes—even if it only stays clean and white for 5 minutes. If you want your baby to display flair and style, don't be too gender conservative. The days of boys just in blue and girls just in pink are over, so enjoy experimenting with color and texture.
* When choosing fabrics, opt for cotton first. Wool is usually too scratchy. Many children's clothing designers now use cashmere/silk/cotton mixes for sweaters that are luxurious yet affordable. Artificial fabrics should be saved for outerwear.

SIZING

You can buy ahead, but there's nothing less fun for a child than wearing all oversized clothes—just like you, children want their clothes to fit. Do buy T-shirts and onesies in a range of sizes so that they can be layered. And when pajamas with socks attached become too small, chop the bottoms off. Also, clothes made of stretchy fabrics are more forgiving and more versatile, and will fit right for longer.

TRICKS

It isn't easy to dress a baby so try to make sure your baby is calm before you begin. A good time for changing is typically after a feeding. Take your time, be patient, and use a changing table or other flat surface so your baby is comfortable.

Our son used to hate putting on pajamas until we turned the process into a game. We would make dressing into a theatrical event by singing to him and pretending he was getting ready for a car race or putting on magic clothes. Dressing with him worked well, too.

Have fun with the "Mommy and me, Daddy and he" concept. Your son and his dad can put on the same white sneakers, blue jeans, and a white T-shirt on a Sunday or your little girl can wear a similar outfit to Mom's.

Never has there been so much choice for babies and kids. If you try to have some fun with your child's clothes, then she or he will as well.

46

WEAR YOUR BABY

MARIA BLOIS

Dr. Maria Blois is the author of Babywearing:

The Benefits and Beauty of This Ancient Tradition.

At some point, usually quite early on, we look down at the tiny bundle in our arms and realize *we are about two hands short for the task.* Tiny babies are exceptionally floppy and often require us to use both hands to hold them properly, leaving no hands free to get anything else done.

One of parenting's best-kept secrets is the art of "babywearing,"[1] the practice of carrying our baby in a soft carrier close to our body as we go about our daily business. After all, who can argue with a happy baby and two free hands? But beyond convenience, babywearing has even more benefits. Studies consistently show that babies who are worn close to their parents' bodies cry less, are more calm and content, sleep more peacefully, nurse better, gain weight better, enjoy better digestion, and develop better.

---

[1] The term *babywearing* is trademarked and used with the permission of Dr. William Sears.

Babywearing also benefits parents. It enhances parent–baby bonding, is practical and stylish, facilitates breastfeeding, helps working parents reconnect, and makes transitions from one caregiver to another easier. From preemies to toddlers, babies of all ages can be worn. Most good soft carriers (depending on the model) can accommodate babies up to forty pounds or so, which means your child will outgrow the need to be carried before he outgrows the actual carrier. Not many baby products can boast such a long life span. And there is no limit to how long you can wear your baby; this is determined by your comfort level. It is best to change sides each time you wear a one-sided carrier (most slings and pouches).

Babies can be worn on your front, side, or back in a variety of soft carriers.

* *Slings* go over one shoulder and around the hip. They are easy to put on and take off, and you can breastfeed easily and discreetly in a sling.
* A *wraparound carrier* is essentially a long piece of fabric that wraps around you and Baby in a variety of comfortable positions. Wraparounds require a steeper learning curve and are a bit more involved to put on and take off, but they are the absolute best for distributing Baby's weight. You may breastfeed discreetly on both sides when carrying Baby in the front.
* *Packs* hold Baby vertically in the front or the back. These types of carriers are a favorite for your back as Baby is supported on both of your shoulders (unlike the sling) and there is less fabric than a wraparound.

To get you started, here are some instructions for using a sling.

1. Hold the sling, tail hanging down, rings in front.

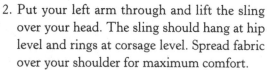

2. Put your left arm through and lift the sling over your head. The sling should hang at hip level and rings at corsage level. Spread fabric over your shoulder for maximum comfort.

3. Find pouch. Locate both the inner rail (always between you and Baby) and outer rail. Each rail can be tightened independently by pulling the corresponding fabric through rings. Make sure the sling is not twisted.

4. Put Baby over your left shoulder as if to burp him. Support him with your left hand.

5. Put your right hand under the sling and gather Baby's feet together.

6. Gently slide Baby into pouch keeping the inner rail close against your body. Fabric must always be between you and Baby. Tuck Baby's feet up into fetal position.

7. Pull outer rail up and over Baby's back. If carrying a tiny newborn, go all the way over Baby's head for more support.

8. Tighten the sling in order to be secure. This is a must!

9. Make sure Baby is completely supported before letting go. Start moving . . .

Whichever type of soft carrier you pick, you and your baby will reap the benefits of this special time together. You will free up your two hands (hallelujah!) and your baby will grow and thrive right next to you.

47

DOCUMENT BABY'S LIFE

LISA BEARNSON

Lisa Bearnson is the founding editor of Creating Keepsakes
scrapbook magazine and the co-author of three books, including
Mom's Little Book of Displaying Children's Art. *She is the*
host of the monthly QVC program Creating Keepsakes Hour.

B efore you know it your baby will be off to college. Then
you'll finally have the time to preserve his memories, but no
memory of your own to do it with. The following are my top tips
for preserving your baby's memories now without adding to your
stress.

Keep a calendar exclusively for your child. This is my number-
one tip, a quick and easy way to keep track of important information and events. It's best to buy one specifically for a baby.
Childhood flies by and you won't remember the exact date when
the little things (like a first smile), or even many of the big ones
(like a first step), took place. Write anything and everything on
the calendar, including milestones, doctor visits with weight and
height, world events, and other special occasions you'll want to
remember later. I suggest doing this for two years.

Invest in a good camera. Be sure to get a camera that can either put a date on the back of the photo or one that codes the date into the file name (digital). Otherwise, write the date on the back of the photo once it is developed or printed. This will be invaluable later! Many of my own childhood photos require me to guess not only my age but also if it was me or one of my sisters!

Take a monthly photo. A fun way to chart growth is to take a photo of your child next to the same toy or stuffed animal on the same day each month. The toy will seem huge in the beginning and small by the end of the first year. This series makes for a great scrapbook layout.

Pick only the best photos. There is no hard-and-fast rule that says you must scrapbook every photo you've ever taken. Scrapbooking will be more enjoyable if you simply pick the best ones and focus on those.

Keep a treasure box. There are many items too big for a scrapbook but too precious to throw out. I recommend getting a plastic box with a tight-fitting lid for each child's keepsakes. Get clasp envelopes of different sizes, or even plastic bags that can be zipped closed for memorabilia, and be sure to label the envelope or bag with the date, what's inside, and why it's significant. For example, for handmade booties, label who made them, when they were worn, and other information you'll want other generations to know about them. You may not be around when they're handed down, and this information will be priceless. I've stored items such as lost teeth, locks of hair, special toys, cards from well-wishers, blankets, and more.

Decide before scrapping. Before beginning your scrapbook, sketch out a pattern for how you want it to look. Choose paper and other embellishments, keeping them consistent throughout the book. Thinking out the specifics beforehand makes putting the book together faster, easier, and more pleasing to the eye.

Journal meaningfully. When you get ready to scrapbook, pull out your calendars to jog your memory. Names and dates are always important on a scrapbook page, but focus on your thoughts and feelings, as if you were actually writing in a journal. A bubble coming out of a child's head with "Aren't I cute?" not only has you stating the obvious, but you'll regret the silliness later! Besides, a baby wouldn't actually think "Aren't I cute," would he? Instead, a separate box with your words about whose eyes the baby has, or how you felt the day your baby was born, is much more meaningful.

Don't be afraid. Stepping outside the box is good—make scrapbooks on different themes or in different sizes. For example, I made my youngest a "Baby's Milestones" book that's only six by six inches in size. Each page is dedicated to a month with one photo and journaling about what she did at that time. This takes less than a day to create, and will give you a great sense of accomplishment! You could also make a book dedicated to the pregnancy and birth or one just about Baby's family.

48

PHOTOGRAPH BABY

Tom Arma

Tom Arma has been called "the world's most published baby
photographer" by the New York Times. *He has published*
thirty-five children's books in addition to his Please Save the
Animals *series of calendars, greeting cards, and other products.*
Arma's newest venture is the Tom Arma Signature Collection,
which will make costumes he designed for his baby
photographs available to the public.

Photographing a baby, whether yours or someone else's, need
not be challenging if you make some preparations. Creating a fun
experience for everyone involved, especially Baby, will ensure a
successful photo shoot.

1. FIND A HELPER. Enlist the aid of a family friend or relative
   whom the baby relates well to. With the help of your new
   assistant, make all of your preparations prior to bringing the
   baby into the room.

2. PREP THE BABY. Dress Baby in something comfortable and
   make sure it is neither too hot nor cold in the room. It is

important that Baby has just been fed or nursed, had her nap, and had a diaper change.

3. USE FAVORITE THINGS. Gather a few of Baby's favorite toys, things she responds to, like rattles or a stuffed toy.

4. CREATE A COMFORTABLE ENVIRONMENT. To create a background, choose a blanket or adult-sized comforter in a pleasing color with no distracting patterns. Lay one side on top of the seat part of a couch and let the rest fall to the floor, pulling the edge toward you and creating a continuous backdrop over the floor for Baby to sit or lie on. If you have hardwood floors place a mat or thick carpet on the floor under the material you choose to make Baby nice and comfy and to cushion an unsteady sitter. Place a small piece of tape on the fabric to mark the spot where Baby will be placed on the "set."

5. CHECK YOUR CAMERA. Make sure it has fresh batteries, the lens is clean, the lens cap is off, and, if it is not a digital camera, that there is film in it. If you want to use your flash attachment check that it's working now. Use the automatic setting. Most modern cameras perform well in this mode. "Waste" a shot to make sure you're all set—it is worth sacrificing one photo to know that your flash and camera are ready for Baby's first smile.

6. MINIMIZE DISTRACTIONS. Aside from you and your assistant, nobody should be visible to the baby during the shoot. Turn off anything that makes noise or is distracting. Work in a quiet room.

7. GET DOWN ON BABY'S LEVEL! This is the key to a great baby photo. Lie on your stomach and place your camera on a flat surface in

front of you. A thick telephone book or two will do nicely. Make sure you are far enough away to fill up your viewfinder with all of Baby, whether she is sitting or lying down.

8. CAPTURE THE ACTION. Now the fun begins! Baby photography is a lot like sports photography in that it is all about being prepared to catch the "moment." Lie down and ready yourself, placing your finger on the shutter release as you look through the viewfinder. Don't lift your head until you get the shot. Have your assistant place the baby on the blanket and quickly get down on the floor, so that the assistant's head is above yours. This way he or she can play peek-a-boo, make funny sounds, or use a favorite toy while you concentrate on capturing the smile that is sure to come.

49

TRACK DEVELOPMENTAL MILESTONES

Alan Greene

Dr. Alan Greene is a pediatrician and author of From First Kicks
to First Steps, *among other books. He sees patients and teaches*
residents at Lucile Packard Children's Hospital at Stanford
University School of Medicine. He was the first pediatric expert
for Yahoo!, Rob Reiner's Parents Action for Children, and the
People's Pharmacy. *His award-winning pediatric website,*
www.drgreene.com, receives over 50 million hits a month.

Unparalleled growth takes place in bursts during the first two
years. To make sense of this dizzying affair, I sort growth into
the following four story lines:

THE APPRENTICE

When a newborn fixes her eyes on something intriguing, she
might swipe toward it with her arms or legs. This is the beginning of her training in hand-eye coordination, which will one day
enable her to master tasks such as tying shoes, playing the piano,
or performing neurosurgery.

From birth, a baby can grasp a finger pressed into her hand. Over time, this behavior will become more precise. Usually, babies first grasp with the little-finger half of the hand and move to the thumb side with practice. At about six months old they'll be passing toys from hand to hand. Next, they start peering at smaller objects as they are about to develop a precise finger-thumb grasp. By twelve months, they are ready to hold objects and build with them. When a baby can build a stack of blocks, or turn a doorknob, the apprentice has completed his journeyman training.

THE ATHLETE
TUMMY TIME

Tummy time begins soon after the umbilical stump has fallen off. This position builds strength and coordination, and offers exercise in head control, baby's first weight-lifting accomplishment, which usually takes place within just twelve weeks. Rolling over follows as the whole body gets into the act.

SITTING

Sitting alone is a major childhood milestone that comes around six months. Babies progress by planting their hands in front of them to create a human tripod. You will see your baby's growing adeptness as her hands come closer to her body as she sits—until one day she lifts up her arms for a few seconds! In just a few more weeks, she will be sitting, twisting, and reaching for objects with easy confidence. Soon your budding athlete launches across the floor on an obstacle course of new discoveries. Many healthy babies never crawl, but they do need to find some way to move across the floor.

STANDING

When babies are able to pull themselves to standing, they feel a sense of triumph along with an urgency to walk. The normal age for first steps ranges from seven months to seventeen months. More than half of babies in the United States start to walk *after* their first birthday. At the moment of that first step, your baby becomes a toddler.

Athletic skill continues to increase in the second year through walking, climbing, and jumping.

THE SCHOLAR

Behind the scenes, your baby is gaining a deep understanding of how things work. While babies are learning to sit, for instance, they also learn to intuitively judge the speed of an approaching object, instinctively calculate the time to collision, and blink at the perfect moment.

Around six months, they may begin to exhibit separation anxiety and stranger anxiety. Both coincide with a new intellectual skill called object permanence. Your baby now remembers objects and specific people who are not present. He doesn't want a stranger, because the stranger is not you.

As with other parts of development, getting mobile changes the way babies think. While your baby is still fascinated by your eyes, she is increasingly focused on where your eyes are looking. Soon your baby is able to hold an image of where things in the room are located, without being able to see or hear them.

As they begin to walk, a new depth of self-awareness emerges. Babies become fascinated with images of themselves, videos, and mirrors.

There is often a second peak of stranger anxiety at about eighteen months, which fades as language skills improve. By eighteen months toddlers can link actions to solve a problem—like using a stick to reach a toy. And before the second birthday scholars will demonstrate maturity through symbolic actions, such as tenderly giving a bottle to a doll.

THE POET

Both sides of the language coin—understanding and speech—develop in tandem, but understanding leads the way at each stage. Young babies make cooing (soft vowel) sounds, then begin to experiment with varying the volume; within several months, they practice varying the pitch. This happens even in children who are completely deaf.

Sometime after the six-month mark, babbling (consonants and vowels mixed together) begins. The amount and quality of babbling vary depending on how well babies hear and how much people speak to them. Soon babbling gives way to jargon, when babies begin to imitate the sounds and tones of adult speech. Around this time, babies begin to point at objects, a key step in language development.

Kids' jargon begins to coalesce into words, using the same sound for the same object repeatedly. This might be "ba" for *ball*. Babies may or may not say their first words before taking their first steps, but they understand some words long before then. Speaking the first fifty or so words often happens slowly. Within the second year your baby will learn to use hundreds of words and combine them in unique ways. Two-word phrases are the hallmarks of two-year-old poets.

THE PARENT DETECTIVE

As parents, you get to solve the ever-changing mystery of what will make your baby smile. If you try to engage your baby in an activity that is beneath her developmental level, she will quickly get bored. If you try to interest her in something that she is not yet ready for, she will become upset. Babies don't tend to cry when they fail but rather when the activity doesn't suit their developmental level. Your task is to find that fun zone of moderate challenge.

50

PROMOTE MOTOR DEVELOPMENT

LISE ELIOT

Dr. Lise Eliot is assistant professor of neuroscience

at the Chicago Medical School of Rosalind Franklin University

of Medicine & Science and author of What's Going On

in There? How the Brain and Mind Develop in

the First Five Years of Life.

Babies have a great advantage over the rest of us: they actually love to move. Babies keep active without any nagging, guilt, drill sergeants, or exercise gurus. If they're awake and alert, chances are they're kicking their little legs, batting their arms, craning their necks, and trying, with every skill they possess, to advance to the next level of mobility. All this activity is no accident, and probably evolved to ensure babies get the hundreds of hours of practice they need to master each new motor skill.

NEWBORNS TO FIVE MONTHS

The challenge is daunting: born helpless and without any voluntary motor control, babies manage to coordinate every part of their bodies by the end of their first year of life. By one month of age, they've logged enough neck-strengthening exercise to support their own heavy heads. By five months, they can finally reach out and successfully grasp an enticing object, like your dangling car keys, a tricky act that requires considerable coordination of vision, arm movement, and a carefully timed grasp.

SIX TO TWELVE MONTHS

Sitting comes next, around six months of age. After many weeks of back- and abdomen-strengthening exercise, enforced by being propped up with pillows or held upright on Mom's hip, they can now balance happily on their own bottoms without toppling over. Nine months is the age of crawling, when, after months of flailing and scooting on their tummies, babies manage to support themselves on four limbs, synchronizing the forward motion of left arm and right leg, then right arm and left leg, as they excitedly motor around the house. Finally, at around twelve months, their exercise nets the ultimate payoff: those first wobbly steps, a miraculous feat of balance, strength, and coordination that is a landmark of human evolution as well as every child's own personal evolution.

HELPING YOUR BABIES GET THE EXERCISE THEY NEED

Stop parking your baby! With so many high-tech car seats, strollers, bouncy seats, electronic swings, and "exersaucers" (a misnomer, since they impede rather than promote the development of strength and balance), babies barely have a chance to move. Imagine being shackled to a La-Z-Boy when what you really want to do is run around the block! Babies today spend much of their day as just another piece of luggage—carried in car seats from car to grocery cart and back again, without even flexing a neck muscle.

Why not carry your child in your arms, a baby carrier, or a backpack? Being carried not only will give her the opportunity to strengthen trunk muscles and practice balance but also brings her closer to your loving voice, face, and comforting, familiar odor.

Take advantage of your child's instinct to move before he acquires the insidious habit of immobility. Hold hands and walk together. This classic method still works. Take both your baby's hands and help him practice stepping across the room. The easiest way to do this is to stand behind him, holding his hands above his head. Better yet, stand in front of Baby and hold his hands as you walk backward. This way, he can also see your excited face.

For babies just on the cusp of walking, play baby Ping-Pong. You and your spouse sit facing each other on the floor a few feet apart. Hold your baby's legs in a standing position and coax her into taking a few steps toward the other parent. Babies love this game and, with two parents encouraging them, get twice the reinforcement to egg them on!

Babyproof early, and proof again often, so that your child is free to explore, without you having to worry about a precious vase or dangerous electrical outlet. Babies need tummy time (to strengthen their upper bodies for rolling over and crawling), low empty cupboards (to crawl in and out of), and smooth-edged coffee tables (to hold on to while "cruising" in preparation for real walking).

Imagine if only it were so easy for adults to get in shape!

51

DO YOGA WITH BABY

HELEN GARABEDIAN

Helen Garabedian is the founder of Itsy Bitsy Yoga and a certified infant developmental movement educator. She is the author of Itsy Bitsy Yoga: Poses to Help Your Baby Sleep Longer, Digest Better, and Grow Stronger.

It is easy and fun to enjoy the calming effects of yoga with your baby. Yoga helps babies sleep longer and better and some poses can turn fussy babies into happy ones within seconds! The tried-and-true poses below have helped thousands of parents calm and bond with their little ones.

The three golden rules of enjoying yoga with babies are:

1. *Pace:* The younger the baby, the slower you move your baby through the pose.
2. *Sing and Do:* This method entails singing along with your actions. This sets the tempo of the movements, builds predictability, engages more learning centers in your baby's brain, and keeps you calm and breathing.
3. *Repetition:* Babies and toddlers learn through repetition and love to do things again!

THE POSES

APANA

Appropriate for babies between six weeks and twenty-four months old, Apana pose is known to relieve gas and constipation.

Sit on the floor with a soft baby blanket in front of you. Rest your baby on her back on the blanket with her feet closest to you. Slide your thumbs under your baby's thighs. Gently rest your fingers on top of your baby's thighs.

1. Slowly lift your baby's knees up toward her chest as you sing the word "in."
2. Continue to sing the word "in" as you hold Baby's knees in toward her chest for 3 to 10 seconds.
3. Slowly lower your baby's thighs down toward the blanket as you sing the word "out."
4. Repeat 3–10 times, but always stop if your baby seems to have had enough.

CORKSCREW

Appropriate for babies between six weeks and twenty-four months old, Corkscrew helps to relieve constipation and diarrhea.

For Corkscrew you will use the same body and hand placement as in Apana pose.

1. Circle your baby's thighs clockwise with both hands. Allow one revolution of your baby's knees to equal the time it takes to sing "Corkscrew."
2. Continue for 5 to 30 seconds.

Note: To relieve constipation circle your baby's thighs clockwise. This traces the intestinal tract, inviting anything that might be clogged or stuck to move on out. To help rid your baby of diarrhea circle her thighs counterclockwise. This massages the intestinal tract in a reverse fashion, urging the contents of the intestines to stay inside, thus allowing more time for binding.

DIVINE DROPS

This pose is appropriate for babies once they can hold their head up independently until nine months old or when they get too heavy for

you to practice safely. Parents can enjoy Divine Drops nearly anywhere. It helps calm a fussy baby.

Stand and place your baby's back against the center of your chest. Reach your right hand underneath your baby's diaper as if you were creating a seat for her tush. With your left hand secure your baby's chin with your thumb and forefinger to maintain her head upright.

1. Place your feet 18–24 inches apart with your toes facing slightly outward. *Mmm (inhale sound).* Inhale deeply, filling your upper body and torso with breath.
2. *Woo (exhale sound):* Exhale, swiftly dropping down into a wide squat while continuing to hold your baby securely to your chest.
3. Repeat 3–10 times or as long as your baby would like to.

ROLIO

Appropriate for babies between 5 and 24 months old, Rolio increases coordination and offers your baby's lower back and internal organs a nice massage.

Rest your baby on her back on the blanket in front of you. Gather and hold your baby's hands and feet together above her belly with both of your hands.

1. Sing the word "roll" as you roll your baby onto her left side.
2. Sing "li" as you roll your baby onto her back (starting position).
3. Sing "o" as you roll your baby onto her right side.

Continue for 5 to 30 seconds and slow down if your baby's head is not aligned with her spine.

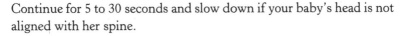

52

READ TO BABY

SUSAN STRAUB

Susan Straub is the founder/director of The Read to

Me Program, Inc., an organization dedicated to connecting

parents, babies, and books. She is a contributor to Family

Literacy: From Theory to Practice *and a co-author of*

Reading with Babies, Toddlers and Twos.

Reading to a baby will be the single most important thing you do with and for your child to prepare him or her for success in school.

Introduce books into your baby's life as early as possible, and be prepared for the reality. Initially, baby "reading" may frustrate eager parents. Babies use all their senses to explore books and at first this will include putting the pages into their drooly mouths. Once babies can use their hands, the reading activity really changes. Now they "read" by manipulating the book, turning it upside down or backward, and using books as toys for stacking, dropping, or passing back and forth. Doing these interactive activities, in fact, still counts as reading and learning about books. Meanwhile, you the parent need to relax and enjoy these

DEVELOPMENTAL LEVEL	ACTIVITY
Newborn	Babies love the sound of your voice. Everything you say stimulates her brain and begins a conversation. At this age, she's every bit as happy to hear *Sports Illustrated* as Winnie the Pooh.
Grasping	Try putting her on the floor with an open book in front of her for "tummy time."
Sitting	Sit on the floor across from your baby and hand books back and forth. Read them and talk about them—"Can I have the book with the doggie? Thank you!"
Crawling or creeping	Action may win over reading for the next few months. If you find yourself struggling to read to Baby, save books for quiet moments, before naps and bedtime. In time she *will* tire, and she *will* need a break (and so will you).
Cruising/Walking	This is a big time for throwing books, too. Books are toys but not balls, so if your child is treating books inappropriately, it's probably time to stop reading and try another game.
Talking (a few words)	Baby may have one favorite word for everything in the book and elsewhere, like *boggie*. Be patient and try distinguishing cat-*boggie*, dog-*boggie*, and Grandma-*boggie*.
Talking more	Now you can open to a page and play "Where is the [choose object]?" Wait for an answer from your child! Be patient—try not to help until she's really stumped. Ask about the less obvious things on the page, too.

early antics. Your baby wants and likes to be with you and to have your attention. And he loves the sound of your voice. Be patient—eventually you'll get to read the whole story.

Reading develops along with the child's capacities to interact and comprehend and it should always be fun. For maximum success and pleasure, focus on what the baby *can* do. The chart on the previous page suggests one book-related activity for each of the baby's developmental stages.

Which book should you start with? *Pat the Bunny* by Dorothy Kunhardt remains an excellent early choice because it entertainingly offers us ways to involve our baby in wonderful activities. It invites babies and parents to respond to the world with their senses, to interact meaningfully and playfully, and leads to more pleasurable shared reading. Other surefire hits for babies up to twenty-four months include *My Aunt Came Back* by Pat Cummings, *Is Your Mama a Llama?* by Deborah Guarino, and *Tickle, Tickle* by Helen Oxenbury. And of course, nursery rhymes are essential.

Once your baby has a favorite book, you'll need to read and reread it multiple times per sitting. And as you go about your daily chores and errands, babies and books can go along, too. Reading the neighborhood signs or playing a kind of I Spy game is good for older ones. Remember: a book in the diaper bag or backpack ensures that you'll never be without entertainment for your little one.

53

INTRODUCE BABY TO MUSIC

DON CAMPBELL

Don Campbell is the author of eighteen books on the
importance of music in health and education. His best-selling
Mozart Effect for Children *books and accompanying CDs*
have been translated into seventeen languages. An advocate
for healthy sound environments, he works with learning
centers, schools, and hospitals worldwide.

Music is a bridge from the head to the body, from the ears to the heart. It is a vital nutrient for building the brain, balancing the body, and giving emotional release so that you can create a healthy psychological state of mind for you and your child.

What your child hears in the first years of life influences language, motor skills, and coordination. The musical diet you provide can build complex neural pathways that will assist your child in multiple tasks throughout life. Silence, storytelling, rhymes, and songs are just a few of the wonderful auditory options that provide health and stimulation to the brain and the body.

Your baby was conceived in a human metronome of pulse, beat, and pattern. Sixteen to twenty weeks after conception, the embryo's eighth cranial nerve begins to eavesdrop on the outer world. The mother's voice as well as other sounds and even music become a part of this sensorial input in the baby's brain and body. In the two months before birth, a parent can compose a song for his baby and sing it to the belly two or three times a day or play a recording at a moderate or quiet volume. The same song will then have a great calming effect after birth. Everything from rocking to patting and cuddling, and the soothing sounds of a parent's lullaby, become the swaddling sounds that create close connections.

About ten days after birth, the baby's ears drain of fluid. This sonic birth to our world may often cause the infant to feel startled and shocked by the sounds. Quiet music is great in the first weeks of life. Have a variety of music available, but there is no need to use it continually. A few times a day is far better than continuous music. Talk and sing in a rhythmic pattern and say your baby's name often.

The voice of Mom and Dad can create both relaxing and playful atmospheres. Whether you are a singer or not, try to "singsong" your voice to nursery rhymes and even for basic activities. A little rhythm and melody helps Baby maintain attention and it serves to improve his vocabulary. For example, take the tune of "Twinkle, twinkle, little star," which is a Mozart melody, and add words like "Let's go riding in the car."

After three months Baby is aware of sound and its source of direction, from the dog barking to fire trucks and televisions. It is the long, low sounds and pretty intervals; easy little tunes; and that "cooing, oohing, and wooing" that instill in a child a sense of safety and curiosity to reach out to the world. Try tapping a plastic spoon on a glass of water, wind chimes, or the happy songs and dances of playtime. All bring stimulation, harmony, excitement, and joy into your baby's life.

FIVE TIPS FOR CREATING A SOUND DIET FOR YOUR BABY'S EARS

1. *Watch out for noise and sound clutter in your baby's room.* This is especially important during the first few months of life. Radio, television, heaters, cell phones, air conditioners, computers, and video games clutter the environment.
2. *Be careful with loud noises.* Your baby may be far more sensitive to sound than you are. Loud noises can startle and shock a baby's system and even damage his hearing.
3. *Music is great for enhancing play.* Use music a few times a day for special activities. Try reading a story with calm music in the background.
4. *Lower and slower sounds help a baby rest.* Slow classical music is perfect for helping a baby sleep and at the same time helping parents release stress. Music that gets progressively slower and softer is ideal.
5. *Silence is as important as sound.* Be sure there are quiet times every day and quiet places so your baby's ears can rest.
6. *Sing messages to your child.* Speak in rhythm. Don't worry about your talent; the highs and lows of your voice are far more interesting with melodies than just normal speech.

Music speaks to multiple areas of the brain all at once. Emotion, movement, speech, and melodic flow offer wonderful ways to build your child's brain and body. From Mozart to your favorite songs, let music constantly nourish your home and family.

54

TEACH BABY TO SELF-SOOTHE

SUZY GIORDANO

Suzy Giordano, aka "the Baby Coach," has trained hundreds of babies to self-soothe and sleep twelve hours a night. She is the author of 12 Hours Sleep by 12 Weeks Old *and* The Baby Sleep Solution: A Proven Program to Teach Your Baby to Sleep 12 Hours a Night.

Self-soothing is a basic teachable skill. It is as necessary and important as learning how to walk, learning how to talk, and other milestones in your baby's mental and physical development. Just as you encourage walking and talking, you should also encourage your baby's self-soothing skills.

Babies who can self-soothe are more willing to play contentedly by themselves and do not require constant entertainment by parents and other caregivers. This contentment will grow later in life. They will be more approachable and more social because they do not have to have their way all the time. Children who have learned to self-soothe will say to themselves, "I don't have to have that toy, I know how to share. I have always shared everything because I am a part of, not the center of, my family."

The ability to self-console also leads to self-control. You may be able to avoid the dreaded screaming toddler meltdown in the supermarket parking lot. In essence, a baby who learns to self-soothe will have a more peaceful and secure journey through toddlerhood.

DOs

1. Do place your baby in the crib at naptimes and bedtime when he is still awake.
2. Do use a pacifier in the crib if needed—just make sure you do not find yourself repeatedly replacing it in your baby's mouth all night long.
3. Do use a musical crib toy and/or an emotional toy or blankie with Mom's scent during naps or nighttime sleep.
4. Do wait a few minutes before going into the nursery if your baby wakes up crying during naps or nighttime sleep. Try not to immediately run into the nursery as soon as you hear your baby cry.
5. Do go into the nursery if your baby is still crying after several minutes and reassure your baby from the side of the crib with a firm touch, a pat on the back, shushing, and whispering, "Everything is all right." Try to avoid taking the baby out of the crib. Also avoid soothing him back to sleep—your goal is to bring your baby down a notch so he will try to calm down on his own again. Exit the room, wait a few minutes, and repeat if necessary.

DON'Ts

1. Do not put your baby in a swing or vibrating chair/bassinet every time he cries.
2. Do not let your baby use the breast or bottle as a soothing tool.
3. Do not interact or make eye contact with your baby during naps or nighttime sleep.

4. Do not clutter the crib. Keep it safe by limiting the amount of toys and allowing the baby to have enough space to move around and find a comfortable sleeping position.
5. Do not immediately go and get your baby out of the crib the moment he wakes up from his nap or nighttime sleep.

Learning to walk involves some stumbling and falling along the way, and learning to self-soothe will involve some pitfalls as well. But just as your child will eventually master the skill of walking with your guidance and encouragement, so, too, will he master the skill of self-soothing.

55

WORK WITH BABY'S TEMPERAMENT

JAN KRISTAL

Jan Kristal is a counselor in private practice and a faculty member of the Department of Psychology at the Dominican University of California, San Rafael. She is author of The Temperament Perspective: Working with Children's Behavioral Styles *and co-author of* The Instructor's Manual for Temperament-based Parenting Classes.

Your baby will approach the world in his own special way. Some babies are happy and easygoing while others present constant challenges. A large part of a child's unique behavior can be explained by understanding his temperament, the innate behavioral style that determines how he responds to the world around him.

Researchers have labeled eight different temperament traits that are identifiable in infancy. Babies have a combination of all of them in varying degrees. Here are the traits and some strategies to help you work with them:

1. SENSITIVITY THRESHOLD (THE LEVEL OF STIMULATION NECESSARY TO EVOKE A RESPONSE)

Sensitive babies protest a dirty diaper and can become easily over-stimulated in busy, noisy environments, while babies low in sensitivity do not mind a dirty diaper and may not indicate an ear infection until the doctor finds it during a routine checkup. *Strategies:* Keep overstimulating environments to a minimum and have quiet times each day to reduce stimulation for your sensitive baby. For babies with low sensitivity, be aware of subtle cues that may indicate an illness or injury.

2. ACTIVITY LEVEL (GENERAL MOTOR ACTIVITY)

Active babies are in constant motion and dislike being confined in a stroller or car seat, while low-activity babies are content to stay put and excel at fine motor skills. *Strategies:* Be careful not to roughhouse with your active baby too close to bedtime, but do provide sufficient ways to express energy throughout the day. Make sure to babyproof when Baby becomes mobile. Low-activity babies will do things more slowly so be patient. Gradually encourage more independence.

3. INTENSITY OF REACTION (HOW EXPRESSIVE BABY IS)

Intense children are loud and expressive whether happy, sad, or angry, while low-intensity babies are quiet and subdued. *Strategy:* When intense babies become upset they need parents to respond calmly. Watch for cues of escalating intensity and use calming activities early.

4. BIOLOGICAL REGULARITY (PREDICTABILITY OF BODILY FUNCTIONS)

Babies who are high in regularity are predictable in eating, sleeping, and elimination patterns, while low-regularity babies vary in their patterns. *Strategies:* For your regular baby, set schedules for eating and sleeping. Low-regularity babies may eventually accept feeding and eating schedules, but if not, don't push it. Try to learn Baby's biological rhythms to gradually move him toward a schedule.

5. ADAPTABILITY (HOW EASILY BABY ADJUSTS TO CHANGE)

Highly adaptable babies easily adapt to different settings and new places, while slow-adapting babies have difficulty adjusting to changes in routine, or moving from one activity to the next. *Strategies:* Don't overlook the needs of highly adaptable babies because of their easygoing nature. Slow-adapting babies do best with structure so be consistent. Make changes and transitions slowly, and give Baby time to adjust. Let Baby know of changes through rituals, songs, and gestures.

6. APPROACH/WITHDRAWAL (BABY'S INITIAL RESPONSE TO NEW THINGS)

Approaching babies have a wonderful curiosity, while withdrawing babies prefer the familiar and reject anything unknown. *Strategies:* Approaching babies need ways to satisfy their curiosity but also need safety precautions. Help withdrawing babies to gradually "warm up" to new people, places, and environments. Use repetition to help familiarize your child with something new.

7. PERSISTENCE (THE ABILITY TO CONTINUE A CHALLENGING ACTIVITY)

Persistent babies repeatedly practice new motor skills and are able to amuse themselves because of their excellent attention spans, while babies low in persistence become easily frustrated. *Strategies:* Choose your battles with a persistent baby and be clear and consistent when responding. Parents can help babies low in persistence to stretch their frustration tolerance by waiting just a bit longer before stepping in to help with a frustrating task. Break frustrating activities into smaller parts and redirect Baby when he becomes too frustrated.

8. DISTRACTIBILITY (HOW EASILY BABY IS DISTRACTED; THE LEVEL OF CONCENTRATION)

Distractible babies are easy to soothe because they can readily shift their attention, while low-distractible babies can intently focus their attention on a task or toy but, if upset, may be difficult to calm. *Strategies:* Use redirection with distractible babies when they get into an undesirable activity. Eliminate surrounding distractions at times when Baby needs to focus, such as during feeding. Try to redirect a low-distractible baby early, and put closure on one activity before moving on to the next.

Understanding your baby's temperament will help you provide care to match your baby's individuality, enabling you to take a proactive approach to work with rather than against your child's personality.

56

GET BABY TO SLEEP
THROUGH THE NIGHT

MARC WEISSBLUTH

Dr. Marc Weissbluth is a pediatrician in private

practice in Chicago. He is the author of

Healthy Sleep Habits, Happy Child.

T he way to get your baby to sleep through the night is to keep him well rested. Sleep-deprived babies have more difficulty falling asleep and staying asleep.

NEWBORN TO SIX WEEKS

When you come home from the hospital you will anticipate when your baby becomes hungry and find a quiet place to feed him; do the same for sleeping. Your newborn will become sleepy within one to two hours of wakefulness so you'll want to find a quiet and dark area to soothe your baby to sleep after this interval. The naps will be brief (twenty to forty minutes long) and irregular. For the first few weeks, your baby will sleep anywhere, but this is only a temporary phase. When your baby needs to sleep, don't take him out in public where there is a lot of noise or stimulating lights. Just as you don't feed on the run, don't nap on the run. At this stage it is impossible to spoil your baby so do whatever works to maximize sleep and minimize crying with your newborn. Use swings, car rides, rocking chairs, swaddling, hugging, holding, soft front carriers, and if your baby sleeps best in motion and not well when put down, use motion.

Your partner should be just as involved in soothing the baby to sleep during the day and at night so that your baby doesn't become dependent on just one of you to do so. After soothing him, put your baby down drowsy but awake so that he learns how to soothe himself to sleep.

SIX WEEKS TO FOUR MONTHS

Anticipate that at six weeks from the baby's due date, there will be a peak of fussiness, gassiness, and wakefulness, especially in the evening. Around six weeks, the bedtime will become earlier so watch for drowsy signs around 6–8 P.M. Avoid keeping your baby up after that even though you want to continue to play with him! Remember, your baby's brain needs sleep for its healthy development just as the body needs food for its growth and development. Healthy sleep occurs in sync with the natural body rhythms so soothe your baby to sleep at the first sign of drowsiness and make the nighttime visits quick and quiet. It's time to feed and change, not play, so there should be minimal soothing. Make sure the intervals of wakefulness during the day are no more than two hours long.

Night sleep begins to lengthen after six weeks of age so there will be four to six hours of uninterrupted sleep, usually occurring before midnight. This is the beginning of the internal biological clock rhythm that creates longer night sleep. If you have an early bedtime when your baby is between two and three months, a predictable and long morning nap (one to two hours) will emerge around 9 A.M. Between a few weeks and a few months later, a predictable and long midday nap (one to two hours) will emerge around 1 P.M. There may or may not be a third nap around 3 to 4 P.M., but this nap is irregular and often brief. These naps and an early bedtime are necessary to produce sleeping through the night.

FOUR MONTHS

By four months, expect to feed your baby either not at all, once, or twice at night. If you are breastfeeding and using a family bed, you might feed more often. The first feeding occurs at least four hours after the last feeding before Baby goes to sleep, and the second feeding occurs around 4 to 5 A.M. Babies do not need to be fed more than twice at night. If you bottle-feed your baby more often, you will create a night waking habit.

Beyond four months of age, continue to feed your child at night as long as you think your child is really hungry. If he sucks eagerly and quickly goes back to sleep, he's hungry. If he sucks slowly and then wants to play, he's not hungry. If he's not hungry, give him less attention at night with extinction (not going to him at all), graduated extinction (waiting five minutes to go to him the first time, ten minutes the second time, fifteen minutes the third time, and so forth), check and console (responding promptly to his first cry but minimally soothing him and preferably not picking him up), or father plus water instead of mother plus breast so that he will learn to sleep better at night. When responding, you should consistently soothe to a calm state or soothe to a sleep state. Children past nine months of age do not need bottles at night for nutrition.

57

TEACH BABY TO NAP

JODI A. MINDELL

Dr. Jodi Mindell is the associate director of the Sleep Center at the Children's Hospital of Philadelphia, a professor of psychology at Saint Joseph's University, and a professor of pediatrics at the University of Pennsylvania School of Medicine. She is the author of Sleeping Through the Night: How Infants, Toddlers, and Their Parents Can Get a Good Night's Sleep *and* Take Charge of Your Child's Sleep. *She is the sleep expert for* BabyCenter.

There are no hard-and-fast rules about naps, but some general guidelines will help your baby get the daytime sleep she needs. During the first few months a newborn will sleep anywhere with no particular schedule. By three months, naps will be more predictable, although every baby is different. Some babies take two naps a day, each an hour or two long. Others will take three or four naps, each thirty to forty-five minutes. It's best to have your baby nap in the same place where she sleeps at night. And it's best to put her in her crib drowsy but awake for all naps. If you start early enough, before problems arise, you can just put your baby down awake in her crib and she is likely to happily fall asleep on her own.

At eight to twelve weeks, you can begin to get your baby on a schedule. At this point, nap times can be by the clock or by the two-hour rule. To put your baby on either schedule, just do it for a week or so, whether your baby seems tired or not. After several days to a week, your baby's body will adjust and will start becoming tired at those times.

If you go according to the clock, set your baby's nap schedule at certain times, such as at 9:30 A.M. and 2:30 P.M. and stick to it every day.

If you go according to the two-hour rule, your baby will take a nap exactly two hours (usually almost to the minute) from when she last woke up. Follow this schedule throughout the day. So if your baby wakes up at 7:10 A.M., her first nap will be at 9:10 A.M. If she sleeps for an hour, her next nap will be at 12:10 P.M.; if she sleeps for two hours, her next nap will be at 1:10 P.M. This schedule means less predictability, but it's amazing how babies get sleepy literally two hours after they last woke up.

By six to nine months, all babies should be napping according to the clock. And by eighteen months, most toddlers switch to one longer afternoon nap.

THE BASIC NAP-TIME METHOD

It can be incredibly frustrating to have a baby who doesn't nap during the day. Not only do babies get cranky, but so do parents. To solve your child's nap-time woes, follow the basic nap-time method:

* *Before Starting:* Establish bedtime and nighttime sleep schedules first. Be sure that your child is able to fall asleep on his own at bedtime and is sleeping through the night.

* *Step 1:* Choose a nap-time schedule. Set your baby's sleep schedule using the clock or the two-hour rule.
* *Step 2:* Develop a nap-time routine that is a mini-version of your bedtime routine. The best schedule is "feed, play, and nap" rather than "play, feed, and nap."
* *Step 3:* Now is the time to teach your child to fall asleep on his own at nap time. This is the hard part. Put your child in his crib or bed while he is still awake, say night-night, and leave the room. Wait. Do a simple checking routine if your child is upset. Go back into his room. Tell him that it is okay. Stay for a brief time, no more than a minute. Be boring. Leave. Wait again. Check again. Repeat. Check on your baby as frequently or infrequently as you wish. How long should you continue if your child doesn't fall asleep? Give it 30–60 minutes. Then go get your baby while announcing, "You must not be tired," and go on with your day. Keep him awake until the next nap time or bedtime. You can also take a 15- to 30-minute break and try again. Don't let your child fall asleep elsewhere. If your child starts falling asleep, even 10 minutes later, announce, "You must be tired," and take him back to his crib.

Whatever the issue, being consistent and sticking to a plan for at least two weeks will solve most nap-time issues.

58

ORGANIZE LIFE WITH BABY

STACY DEBROFF

Stacy DeBroff is founder of Mom Central and the
author of the best-selling The Mom Book: 4,278 of Mom
Central's Tips for Moms *and* Mom Central: The Ultimate
Family Organizer.

T ake comfort in the fact that there has yet to be a completely organized parent with a baby. The key to maintaining an organized life is to make use of those free ten- or fifteen-minute breaks during the day while your baby is entertained. Unlike the world of business, your life with a baby does not come with a great deal of prearranged support, established systems, training sessions, meetings, mentors, or structured work flow. But there are some creative solutions that will help things run smoothly.

GETTING OUT THE DOOR

Dreading the task of getting themselves and their babies out the door, many new parents resign themselves to living as prisoners in their own homes. Instead, you can streamline the pre-outing process and resume your role as a full-fledged member of the outside world:

* Keep an emergency diaper bag in the car stocked for last-minute trips. Restock your regular diaper bag immediately upon returning home so you are never caught without the essentials.
* To keep your baby entertained in the car, affix removable stickers to the windows and attach toys to the car seat; rotate them regularly to keep things interesting.
* If your child uses a pacifier, pin an extra to the inside of your purse so you always have one handy.
* To make grocery shopping easier, organize your list according to aisle so you can get in and out quickly. Keep a copy of your grocery list of staple items in the car so you can run in and stock up quickly if you have an extra fifteen minutes while out running errands.

GETTING ORGANIZED AROUND THE HOUSE

* Invest in a hands-free headset so you can catch up on important phone calls or chat with friends while nursing or tending to your baby.
* Set up a second changing area close to where you spend the most time with your baby so you won't have to run up and down the stairs for multiple diaper changes during the day.
* Keep frequently used items, like keys and diapers, in places where you can reach them without stooping or struggling—when you have a screaming baby in your hands, you'll be glad you did.
* Separates, such as pants, jumpers, or coveralls that snap at the crotch, give you the option of changing a dirty item without putting a whole new outfit on your baby, saving you time and keeping laundry from taking over your home.
* Hang a shoe bag with see-through plastic compartments on the wall behind your changing table to store diaper changing toys, ointments, undershirts, and socks for quick reach.

* To minimize your mounting pile of outgrown baby clothes and avoid clutter, host a clothes-swapping party. Invite friends and family to bring outgrown clothes, have everyone sort them into piles by size, and let the swapping begin! Donate any leftovers to a local charity.
* Keep a few emergency eight-ounce cans of formula in your house. That way you'll have them on hand if you become ill and unable to breastfeed, or if the fridge breaks and your entire supply of pumped milk curdles while you are away from your child.
* When you're planning a visit to your pediatrician, ask for the first appointment of the morning or the first one after lunch; at these times your doctor is more likely to be running on schedule.

Lastly, remember that there are plenty of tried-and-true organizational quick fixes to help restore your sanity over the next eighteen years!

59

CARE FOR A TODDLER AND A NEWBORN

MOLLY GOLD

Molly Gold is CEO and founder of Go Mom !nc., a company

dedicated to providing time management methods and products

for mothers. She is the creator of the Go Mom! Planner. She

serves as an expert on scheduling issues for BlueSuitMom.

Before you succumb to the overwhelming reality that you are now doubling your parental workload, have faith. As with all life changes, there will be bumps—occasionally even mayhem—that require skillful navigation. Sometimes you'll handle it well; other times you'll simply survive the day.

FOR TODDLERS: STAY ON SCHEDULE AND ASK FOR HELP

If you remember that most everyone does better with a schedule, your toddler will thrive. Honor your routine as best you can and keep attending to the little things that make your toddler's world go round. If you take a daily walk in the park, make that your one goal for the day. Gradually begin to direct your baby's naps, meals, and play time to coincide with your toddler. Protect your toddler's nap time, be more flexible with where Baby sleeps, and remember that being both hungry and tired is never a good combination, so mind the clock for those simple necessities.

For the initial downtime when you can't leave the house much, stock up on a variety of low-maintenance activities you can easily manage while caring for your newborn. Refresh your supplies of crayons, paper, stickers, books on tape, and videos to fill the gaps when you can't be as hands-on as you would like.

Many toddlers love to help around the house because it makes them feel grown up. Harness this energy to your benefit and you will delight in the sense of accomplishment that radiates from your child. Praise him for being Mommy's helper while carrying lightweight items in from the store or bringing you the changing basket for the baby's diaper. Pick daily tasks he can look forward to doing such as getting the napkins out for mealtime or laying out his pajamas and towel at bath time. In boosting his self-esteem you will also begin to lay the groundwork for additional lessons in independence and resourcefulness.

Take your relatives and friends up on their offers to help by having them watch the baby so you have some one-on-one time with your toddler. Schedule an extra set of hands to help with the baby while you take your toddler to the weekly story time at the library or a music class.

Let anyone who offers make you dinner as often as they want. Your toddler still needs to eat three meals a day and any help you can get in the evening is a gift like no other. They don't call it the witching hour for nothing!

FOR BABIES: ENJOY THE MOMENT

Simple as it sounds, when it comes to the baby, you've been here before. Though you may have forgotten some of the basics, you can never tire of the joy you find in the new life unfolding before you. Make the most of little moments you have to connect with this baby. Hold her often, and if she tolerates it well, use a baby carrier as early as you can to free your hands to help with your toddler.

Know from the start that you will never take as many pictures of your second child as you did with your first, but that's okay. Keep a camera and video equipment close at hand. Stock your diaper bag and car with disposable cameras to capture the unplanned moments. If you choose to keep baby journals, store them in a main traffic location so you can note things as they occur.

Having a positive attitude and sense of humor can be the deciding factor in how we feel about facing new challenges in our lives. When you are sleep deprived and can't seem to put on a smile, force yourself to find one good thing in each day. Maybe you read a story to your toddler at bedtime or noticed your flowers started to bloom in your garden, or you were only fifteen minutes late to the doctor instead of thirty minutes like last time.

At any given moment, you have all your children will ever need within your reach—your love and commitment to raise them well!

60

ACHIEVE BALANCE AS A NEW PARENT

MIMI DOE

Mimi Doe is the founder of Spiritual Parenting, a spiritual retreat for parents on the web. She has written five books for families, including Busy but Balanced, *and was the recipient of the Parent's Choice Approved Seal and a finalist for the Books for a Better Life Award.*

The baby has arrived and your days are jammed. You feel indescribable joy but also a growing anxiety as you struggle to balance the baby's needs with the other demands of your life. From doing the dishes to walking the dog, emptying the diaper pail, getting the shirts dry-cleaned, and writing thank-you notes, life's tasks are beginning to put you over the edge.

Don't panic! It is possible to create harmony within your everyday life. There is no need to move to a Vermont commune. The essential ingredient is balance. Balance allows you to savor your family and enjoy your life instead of breathlessly marching through it.

The following seven tips will bring you closer to achieving balance as a new parent:

1. BE A PERFECTIONIST NO MORE. Give yourself a break and stop fretting about what you can't change or what hasn't gotten done yet. Perfection is impossible for anyone but particularly for a new parent. You are nurturing a new life that you've co-created, a miracle that you've been privileged to harbor—a monumental job—so go easy on yourself. There will be no grades, no promotion, no gold stars for this task. Relax. Even if you've been obsessed with orderly closets your entire life, let them go for a while.

2. GO WITHIN. Amid the whirl that is often your life with a baby, you can truly retreat, even for a moment, to that core of serenity within. Create little habits that calm you. Maybe when the phone rings it is your cue to take a deep breath and release your shoulders. Pour yourself a glass of ice water and put your feet up when you feed the baby.

3. WELCOME A NEW PLAN. You might not travel on luxurious vacations or hike the entire Appalachian Trail right after you have a baby. You *can*, however, experience the essence of those experiences that balance you. Spend an hour alone doing something you love, dance with the baby in the backyard, or hike local conservation land with Baby snug in your carry-pack while continuing to plan lifelong goals and dreams.

4. FUEL UP. Many of us are guilty of skipping lunch and grabbing whatever is handy when hunger strikes—but this rarely provides enough great fuel for our bodies. When we eat healthy with lots of protein, fruits, and veggies, we feel more stable emotionally—

more capable, more resilient. So make it a priority to sit down for lunch, even if it's with babe in arms.

5. CREATE A CLEAN SWEEP. About 30 percent of the "stuff" in our homes is no longer used—outdated clothing, toys with missing pieces, expired items in our medicine cabinets. Clutter kills serenity. It can cause you to feel out of control, a sense of heaviness, depression, and even exhaustion. Set aside a special "create order" day. Buy trash bags and storage bins in fun colors. Put your baby down for a nap, play your favorite music, throw open the windows, and begin to declutter just one room. When you're done, celebrate and begin planning the next room to tackle.

6. DO IT YOUR WAY. There's no "right way" to run your household. You can construct your own way of doing things. A friend of mine just had her fourth daughter. Sorting socks was the chore that drove her crazy. So she bought twenty-five pairs of identical white socks. Her daughters now grab two socks from the clean pile and they always match—problem solved. Another mom I know does one chore a day and by the end of the week it all gets done.

7. PRACTICE THE THREE-QUARTERS RULE. Rather than stressing when the empty gas-tank light pops up on your dashboard, fill the tank when it's three-quarters empty. Same goes for replenishing staples in the pantry. And consider doing laundry and paying bills before you absolutely need to. No more dashing out at midnight for a gallon of milk, searching for clean crib sheets, or fending off the overdue bill calls.

61

CHOOSE BETWEEN WORKING AND STAYING HOME

WENDY SACHS

Wendy Sachs is the author of How She Really Does It:

Secrets of Successful Stay-at-Work Moms.

M ost of us entered into motherhood largely blindfolded. We had no clue about the cocktail of maternal hormones that would surge through and transform us forever—wreaking havoc not only on our bodies but on our brains. We weren't prepared for the conflicting feelings of passion, frustration, love, and even indifference we would feel toward these creatures who grew inside of us. And we certainly were never prepared for how this major life-altering, mind-numbing, body-morphing event would affect our careers.

The media often depict the "good moms" as those who have selflessly given up their careers to be the omnipresent, nurturing, forever patient, fulfilled Super Women who happily shuttle their offspring to music, gym, art, and Mandarin classes before they can even walk.

Most women financially have to keep working after they have children and some women simply feel more fulfilled by continuing to work. If you fall into this category, don't feel that you are a lesser mother and don't apologize for working. Embrace your status as a stay-at-work mom. Studies show that the happiest moms are those who have careers aside from raising their children. Not only does having a career make these women feel better about themselves, but by having the ability to contribute to the household income, many of them felt their status as working moms added to a sense of equality in their marriage.

Whether by need or choice, you might be a stay-at-work mom. Here are some secrets to success:

1. Finding excellent child care is critical to your peace of mind. When you feel that your children are happy, stimulated, and loved, it will make going to work much easier.
2. Don't take on all of the household responsibilities yourself—delegate! A helpful partner, extended family, or hired help is critical.
3. Take control. Having some flexibility or control over your work schedule is essential to integrating career and family. The happiest working moms are those who have predictable schedules and some degree of flexibility.
4. Let yourself off the hook. Your kids don't care if you're perfect; they just want your time.
5. Set boundaries between work and home. If you're checking your e-mail while reading *Goodnight Moon* to your kids, you're letting work and the power of technology interfere with your home life. If you are truly present when you are with your kids, you'll feel less guilty when you are not able to be with them.

For those mothers who have the luxury of choosing between being a stay-at-work mom or a stay-at-home mom, the choice itself creates anxiety. All of us want to be present, engaged mommies, but we want to have an independent identity as well.

These days many new moms who can afford to step out of the workforce are choosing to stay at home while their children are young. If you decide to take some time off, then cherish the opportunity and don't feel guilty for doing so. Remember, our careers are long but our children are only babies once.

Or you might feel it is more important to be home when your kids are in middle school or high school. The benefits of leaving the workforce when your children are older is that you will have had the opportunity to build a more secure financial future, gain seniority at work, and establish a strong reputation. A long track record and good contacts can make it easier to reenter the workforce down the road.

Most women want to be working in some capacity after they become moms. Yes, many want to take a sabbatical from their careers, or they want a reduced workweek, but they still want to keep the door open. Exiting the workforce is easy; reentering is much harder. It is important to keep your professional networks alive. Let former colleagues know where you are and what you are doing. Volunteer your time in your community or in your children's schools, not just by licking envelopes but also by taking on true leadership roles. The best way to fill in traditional career gaps on your résumé is by showing real involvement in philanthropic, community, or civic organizations.

Creating work/life balance is very individual. We each have personal tipping points, and what feels right for one mother simply may not work for another. Today more women than ever weave in and out of careers, stepping out temporarily, switching gears, and changing careers. Ignore the judgment and white noise of the world telling you how a "good mother" behaves. And remember that any decision you make does not have to be permanent. As former secretary of state and mother of three Madeleine Albright has famously said, "Women's lives don't go in a straight line; they zigzag all over the place."

62

RETURN TO WORK

Maria Bailey

Maria Bailey is the founder of BlueSuitMom, a website and magazine for working mothers, and host of Mom Talk Radio.

Y ou waited nine months to hold your baby in your arms and now it's time to leave your bundle of joy for the majority of the day. Dealing with the emotions as well as the increased workload can be a challenge for new mothers. However, preparing for your return to work just as you prepared for the arrival of your new baby can make the transition less overwhelming.

OVERCOMING GUILT

Guilt ranks high among the flood of emotions a mother feels when she decides to head to the office while many of her peers choose to remain home with their babies full-time. Some moms feel resentment if finances dictate their decision to work while others develop jealousy toward child-care providers who get to witness their baby's firsts.

The best way to deal with these emotions is to focus on the positive aspects of your work. As your child grows, he or she will watch firsthand as you pursue your dreams and achieve your goals. Your dedication to balance work and family will set the foundation for your child's own work ethic in school and in the workplace for years to come.

ARRANGING CHILD CARE

Finding the best child-care provider for your child will go a long way toward helping you feel comfortable with returning to work. It may appear to be a Herculean task, but remember that millions of mothers find a source of good child care each year.

PLANNING FOR FEEDING

If you are breastfeeding your baby, you will need a plan for supplying your infant with breast milk. Consult with your employer about the availability of a lactation room or other area that facilitates pumping milk. You will need to borrow or buy a breast pump for the office and devise a system for transporting the milk between work and home. If you decide to introduce formula, do so a few weeks prior to returning to the office.

PREPARING MEALS

After a long day away from your baby, the last thing you want to do is become trapped in the kitchen. Plan and prepare meals on the weekend. By roasting a chicken on Sunday and stirring up a pot of pasta sauce, you can have ready-to-eat meals for those nights you come home tired. Remember to always double any recipes you cook and freeze half for later.

PRIORITIZE YOUR TIME

When it comes to housework, learn to pick your battles. Decide where you are willing to cut corners in caring for your home. Examine your priorities against how you spend your time. If there are chores that you just can't live without completing, try hiring a neighborhood teenager to help. Teens are typically eager to earn extra money and can take anything from mowing the lawn to wrapping holiday presents off your plate, hence freeing your time up for Baby.

COMMIT TO YOUR WORK

Your employer may need reassurance that you will be just as productive upon your return as you were before your maternity leave. Now is a good time to reaffirm your commitment to your job. Educate yourself on the work/life benefits your company offers. If you wish to explore a flexible work schedule such as telecommuting or flex-time, approach your employer after you have drawn out a concise plan complete with goals, time lines, and a built-in trial period.

TAKE TIME FOR YOURSELF

Finally, an often overlooked aspect of balancing work and family— you! Moms work so hard to raise healthy and happy children, forgetting that our children's sense of well-being mirrors our own. Without a happy and healthy mother, there can be no happy and healthy family. Take a few minutes every day to do something for yourself. When your family sees the value you put on your well-being, they, too, will value the effort it takes to balance work and family.

63

ADJUST TO LIFE AS A STAY-AT-HOME PARENT

DARCIE SANDERS AND MARTHA M. BULLEN

Darcie Sanders and Martha M. Bullen are co-authors of
Staying Home: From Full-Time Professional to Full-Time
Parent *and* Turn Your Talents into Profits.

So you're home—now what? As a professional turned at-home mom or dad, you'll face more adjustments than learning how to care for a baby. If you've been in the workforce for several years, you may experience a difficult transition in giving up your title, salary, and professional accomplishments for family life.

Whether you decide to stay home right after the birth of your first child or when your children are older, at-home parenthood requires significant trade-offs. Many parents speak of the culture shock they experienced when moving from the workplace to the home. Their new occupation includes chaotic, disorganized schedules, irregular work hours (with plenty of overtime), no clear job assignments, no performance reviews, mundane chores, and, obviously, no salary. It can take a year or more to get used to a change of this magnitude.

After surveying 300 mothers across the country, we compiled these four ground rules to help you achieve satisfaction and success in your new role.

1. KNOW WHAT YOU WANT YOUR NEW JOB TO BE. When thinking about your work as a home-based parent, remember that your number-one job is caring for your child, not for your house. Don't assume that now that you're home, you're automatically the chief cook and bottle washer—as well as chief diaper changer, housecleaner, chauffeur, and personal shopper. When you and your spouse both worked for pay, you probably shared household chores. There's no reason to discontinue that arrangement now.

   The happiest parents we encountered shaped their role into one that fit comfortably with their own personality and aspirations. You have the opportunity to set your own priorities. If you'd rather take your kids on field trips than do housework, that's your decision.

2. ACKNOWLEDGE YOUR SKILLS. Many at-home parents worry that their professional talents and interests will disappear once they leave the office. The conventional wisdom is to "keep your hand in" by maintaining your professional memberships, doing volunteer work in your area of interest, and taking on part-time projects or consulting. This is good advice. But we have found that just as important as maintaining your work skills is *acknowledging* your skills in your new role. In fact, most of your hard-earned skills can be transferred to your new life at home.

3. SET REALISTIC GOALS. Goal setting—for yourself, your children, your family, and your home—is one of the most important tools you can use to make your life more manageable. Yet many parents

find the often-recommended daily "To Do" lists frustrating. Sick children or rebellious toddlers may prevent you from accomplishing what you'd hoped to do. By creating a more realistic weekly or monthly list of goals, you can get a grip on your life without undermining yourself.

4. FIND A SUPPORT NETWORK. Isolation is the most common problem that at-home parents face. To avoid feeling cut off from the rest of humanity, it's crucial that you find a support network. We all need encouragement from one another and someone to talk with about our daily frustrations, joys, and challenges. Since your old network of colleagues and friends may not be up to the task, make an effort to get out of the house and connect with like-minded parents.

Finally, don't forget to take time out for yourself. Like every worker, you have a right to time off to relax, meet with friends, and pursue your own interests. If hiring babysitters or a nanny is not in your budget, consider swapping playdates with a friend or joining a babysitting co-op. Give yourself permission to have a life of your own—you'll be happier for it, and so will your family.

64

CHOOSE A CHILD-CARE OPTION

ANN DOUGLAS

Ann Douglas is the author of The Mother of All® Pregnancy

Books *and numerous other pregnancy and parenting best sellers.*

So you're planning to head back to work in a few months' time. There's no time like the present to start pounding the pavement in search of affordable, quality child care.

WHAT'S ON THE CHILD-CARE MENU?

The first thing you need to decide is what type of child care would be best for your baby. Each of the four basic choices has its own pros and cons.

1. HAVE SOMEONE CARE FOR YOUR CHILD IN YOUR HOME (A NANNY OR OTHER IN-HOME CHILD-CARE PROVIDER). This may not be your cheapest option, but when it comes to convenience, it beats the other options hands down. You don't have to get Baby into his car seat at 7 A.M. so that you can get to work. On the downside, you've got the joy of cutting through the government red tape that goes along with being an employer. You've also got to pick up the tab for a smorgasbord of

employment taxes. But for families who can afford it, this is truly the mother of all child-care options.

2. HAVE SOMEONE CARE FOR YOUR CHILD IN HIS OR HER HOME (FAMILY DAY-CARE PROVIDER). Because family day-care providers typically work in isolation, you and the other parents will function as their supervisor. But a lot of parents love this option: it's more affordable than nanny care, and it still allows your baby to be cared for in a family-like setting.

3. HAVE YOUR CHILD CARED FOR IN A DAY-CARE CENTER. If reliability is a key factor in determining your choice of child-care arrangements, a day-care center may be your best bet. They will handle the problem if a staff member calls in sick as opposed to other types of child-care arrangements where you have to scramble for backup or miss a day of work. The downside is that there are many children under the same roof, providing a greater opportunity for little ones to swap the virus du jour. And your baby is going to have to share her child-care provider with a lot of other kids—something that would be less of a problem in a family day-care situation and a nonissue if she had Nanny all to herself.

4. HAVE A RELATIVE CARE FOR YOUR CHILD. Asking Grandpa or Aunt Susan to provide care for your child has become such a common practice that it's even earned its own name—relative care. In some families it works out beautifully, in other families, not quite as well. In the end you may decide that it's cheaper to do business with a stranger than to risk destroying a relationship with a relative. Of course, if Grandma and Grandpa have been begging you for the chance to take care of their grandchild since the moment

the pregnancy test came back positive, you may have lucked out and found your way to child-care nirvana.

The top five things to look for when checking out an out-of-home or nonrelative child-care arrangement (family day care or child-care center) are as follows:

1. Accreditation through the National Association for the Education of Young Children (www.naeyc.org), the National Association for Family Child Care (www.nafcc.org), or the National Child Care Association (www.nccanet.org). The minimum health and safety standards set by each state shouldn't be mistaken for a bona fide quality guarantee.
2. Staff with appropriate training and experience (see above).
3. Family-friendly policies and procedures (e.g., how they handle sick children, discipline).
4. A safe and clean environment (pay attention to diaper change, food preparation, and sleep areas; indoor and outdoor play areas; and the entry points to the facility).
5. References from both past and current families.

Remember that your job as a day-care detective is ongoing. You should continue to monitor the quality of care. Pick up your child a few minutes early one day, or drop by in the middle of the day. That's the best way to keep tabs on the quality of your baby's care.

65

INTERVIEW A BABYSITTER OR NANNY

MICHELLE LaROWE

*Michelle LaRowe is the founder and president of Boston
Area Nannies, Inc., a nonprofit educational organization
dedicated to the in-home child-care industry. A career nanny
specializing in twins for the past eleven years, she is the 2004
International Nanny Association Nanny of the Year and the
author of* Nanny to the Rescue!: Straight Talk and Super
Tips for Parenting in the Early Years.

The wind will rarely guide someone who is practically perfect
to your doorstep to care for your most prized possession.
Whether you hear about a child-care provider by word of mouth,
through a placement agency, or even by placing your ad (gulp) on
the Internet, one thing is for sure—if you want to discern Mary
Poppins from Scary Poppins, you have to do your homework.

INTERVIEWING 101
THE PHONE INTERVIEW

Once you've spread the word that you're on the hunt for a caretaker, get your notebook handy and leave it by the phone. Or you can make an application and have printed copies with space for the following:

* Contact information
* Eligibility to work legally in the United States
* CPR and first-aid certifications
* Driver's license
* Highest level of education completed
* Child development or child safety courses taken
* Their description of their personality and interests
* Experience working with children before and in what capacity
* Best child-care experience
* Worst child-care experience and how they handled it
* Their own family life (e.g., number of children, ages)
* What appeals to them about working with children
* How they discipline children
* Three references
* Rate and availability

Tip: While interviewing candidates, save time by screening your calls. Change your voice mail to say something like: "Greetings. If you are calling about our child-care position, please leave a detailed message, including your name, phone number, an overview of your child-care experience, and the best time to reach you." This will weed out those who may not want to answer all of your questions and those who are unable to follow your basic instructions.

THE REFERENCE CHECK

If you've decided to hire a caregiver without the help of an agency, you must be willing to invest the time and energy to contact each reference provided. Ask for one personal reference and two references related directly to his or her child-care experiences. Be ready to ask the following questions:

* How long have you known the candidate? In what capacity?
* What strengths does the candidate have? Weaknesses?
* Do you have any reservations about recommending this candidate?
* Do you still have a working relationship? If not, why?
* Would you employ the candidate again? Why or why not?
* Do you have anything additional to add about this candidate?

Tip: While checking references from past employers, approach the conversation in a relaxed, personal tone. Read between the lines to discern if the reference is enthusiastic or hesitant.

A FACE-TO-FACE MEETING

If you've made it through the phone interview and the reference check and have found some candidates you like, set up a time for them to visit. Watch, listen, and learn. Consider the following:

* Is their appearance neat?
* Do they look you in the eyes when they talk?
* Are they friendly and comfortable around your kids?
* Do they wash their hands before handling your baby?
* Do they seem genuinely interested in your children?
* Do they get on the floor to interact with young ones?
* Do they ask get-to-know-you questions to an older child (e.g., "Can you tell me about your favorite book?")?

Tip: They call it mothers' instinct for a reason. Go with your gut.

A TRIAL DAY

If you liked what you heard over the phone and what you saw in person, called all of the references, and received positive feedback, set a trial day to observe the candidate in action with your child. At the end of the day ask yourself if you liked what you witnessed.

Tip: Run out to do an errand and pop back in unexpectedly.

THE RIGHT HIRE

At the end of the day, if you are confident that you are getting what was presented to you and what you were looking for, then you are ready to make the hire.

66

HELP BABY DEVELOP A SECURE ATTACHMENT

JUDE CASSIDY AND BERT POWELL

Jude Cassidy is professor of psychology at the University of Maryland. She is co-editor of the Handbook of Attachment *and co-editor of the journal* Attachment and Human Development. *Bert Powell is co-creator of the Circle of Security Project, an educational and intervention program for parents and young children. He is also a psychotherapist in private practice at Marycliff Institute in Spokane, Washington.*

S ecurely attached babies have confidence that their parents will consistently respond with affection to their signals for attention, comfort, holding, and exploration. Babies develop this confidence from the way their parents care for them. You'll have countless opportunities every day—twenty times before breakfast—to let your baby know, "I'm here when you need me, and you're worth it." Here are some things to keep in mind:

1. BABIES NEED TO BE HELD. Babies soak up affection through their skin. Gentle touch provides the tenderness every infant requires. Playful touch encourages joy. Soothing touch helps calm a distressed baby.

2. WHENEVER POSSIBLE, RESPOND TO YOUR BABY'S SIGNALS. Babies give signals (big and small) for what they need. Watch for and respond sensitively to these signals, and your baby's security will grow.

3. PICKING UP A CRYING BABY WON'T LEAD TO SPOILING. Some people believe that you will spoil your baby if you pick him up when he cries. In fact, researchers have discovered that children whose parents responded quickly to their crying when they were babies are less demanding and more self-reliant than other children.

4. STAY WITH YOUR BABY DURING DIFFICULT TIMES. Babies often feel sad, hurt, angry, or scared. They can't yet manage intense feelings on their own. To help your baby at these times, stay with her. Touch or hold her until she is calm again. Your baby will learn to trust you; she'll feel, "Someone is here with me when I am in difficulty and pain" and "When Mommy (or Daddy or Grandma) is here, I know that I will feel better soon."

5. HAVE FAITH IN YOURSELF. All parents feel uncertain at times about how to give their baby what he needs. When you are pacing at 3 A.M. with an intensely crying baby, you may understandably feel incompetent, frustrated, and useless. Have faith that your actions are in fact useful because they tell your baby "I can't always make everything better, but I can be with you when you're upset." The baby learns: "When I struggle, I don't have to struggle alone."

6. HAVE FAITH IN YOUR BABY'S TRUST IN YOU. Your baby gains security and confidence in her relationship with you from repeated positive experiences. There is no evidence that the decisions you make about issues like whether or not to breastfeed, whether or not to use day care, and whether or not to co-sleep will affect your baby's security. Make decisions that work for you, your baby, and your family. Your relationship with your baby is what counts.

7. MISTAKES HAPPEN AND YOU DON'T NEED TO BE PERFECT. Perfection is impossible in parenting. In fact, it isn't even recommended. A parent who focuses on perfection can't focus as well on the baby. Fortunately, babies are forgiving. By the time she becomes a toddler, a child who knows that everyone in the family makes mistakes, and that these mistakes will eventually be worked out, will feel more secure than a child who thinks everything has to be right the first time.

8. "I AM HERE WHEN YOU NEED ME, AND YOU'RE WORTH IT." To raise a secure baby you simply need to say these words. The trick is that you need to say them with your heart, your mind, your eyes, your hands, and your behavior. And you need to say them more times than you can count. Babies whose repeated daily experiences lead them to believe the truth of these words will be securely attached.

67

TEACH BABY TO SIGN

LINDA ACREDOLO AND SUSAN GOODWYN

Linda Acredolo and Susan Goodwyn are the co-authors of three

parenting books, including Baby Signs: How to Talk with

Your Baby Before Your Baby Can Talk. *They are co-founders*

of Baby Signs, Inc., a company dedicated to

helping parents teach their babies to sign.

There's nothing more heart-wrenching than hearing your baby cry and not knowing what's wrong. Now, thanks to a growing awareness of how easily babies can learn to communicate with signs, parents are finding it easier to figure out what's on their baby's mind.

Our two decades of research have shown that far from hindering verbal development, encouraging babies to sign actually *speeds up* learning to talk. Just as crawling is a helpful precursor to walking, signing is a helpful precursor to talking.

IT'S AS EASY AS TEACHING BYE-BYE

Parents have actually been teaching their babies to sign ever since the first parents taught their babies to shake their heads for "no," nod for "yes," and wave a hand for "bye-bye." The process of teaching any sign is the same.

First, there's an event that makes saying "bye-bye" appropriate—like Grandma leaving. You get your baby's attention and say something like, "Look, Morgan, Grandma's leaving." Then, as you say the words, "Say bye-bye! Bye-bye Grandma!" with great emphasis, you wave your own hand in an exaggerated manner and perhaps even gently wave the baby's hand. After the baby has witnessed enough of these episodes, the lightbulb comes on and she waves bye-bye herself.

Let's take a look at what is going on here:

> *Your* eyes *looked back and forth between Baby and Grandma.*
> *Your* hands *waved and helped the baby wave.*
> *Your* voice *said "bye-bye" in an exaggerated fashion.*
> *Your* face *expressed enthusiasm!*

Teaching signs is that easy. Let's try it out with the sign for "eat." Little Morgan is sitting in her stroller out in the park and starts to whine. First, you get down to her level and get her attention. Then you say, "Morgan, are you hungry? Would you like something to *eat?*" Every time you say "eat," you also model the sign for "eat" (fingertips tapping lips). Finally, you offer her some Cheerios.

Whether or not Morgan was hungry, you have started to teach her that *if* she is hungry, she can let you know by tapping her fingers against her lips like you did. Repeat this consistently whenever you say the word "eat" to her, and eventually she'll catch on.

TIPS FOR SIGNING SUCCESS

1. *Start modeling signs at six months.* You can start anytime but remember that it can take until after the first birthday or later for a baby to start signing back. Because some babies do start signing

at six months, however, that's when we recommend parents begin.

2. *Start with just a few.* Start with just a few really helpful signs— not because you might overwhelm your baby if you try teaching more, but because the more signs you model, the harder it is for you to remember to model them consistently.

3. *Start with mealtime signs.* Since getting fed is a critical issue in even a young baby's life, mealtime signs are good ones with which to start. In addition to "eat," popular ones include "more" (fingertips of both hands tapped together); "milk" (fist open and closing as though milking a cow), which can also be used for "nursing"; and "drink" (curved hand, thumb to lips).

4. *Always use the sign and word together.* Unless the child has a hearing problem, the ultimate goal is to learn to say words. The signs are mainly a stop-gap measure to minimize frustration until words are available. Therefore, it's very important that the child *hear* the words that go with the signs.

5. *Repetition is the key to success.* The more frequently a child sees a sign, the more likely he or she is to learn it.

6. *Make learning signs a game, not a chore!* Happy babies are likely to learn. Babies who feel pressured, tired, or frightened do not. Teach signs as a natural part of everyday interactions with your baby rather than during structured "lesson times."

68

TAKE BABY TO A RESTAURANT

OLI MITTERMAIER AND ELYSA MARCO

Oli Mittermaier and Dr. Elysa Marco are the founders of

the lilaguides, *pocket-sized guides offering parent reviews*

on everything from baby gear to baby-friendly activities,

stores, and restaurants.

Going out to eat with a squirmy infant or curious toddler is easier than it sounds and it gets easier the more you do it. Here are some pointers taken from parents who not only eat out with their kids but also enjoy it.

FIND THE RIGHT RESTAURANT

There are some restaurants that cater to parents and some that would rather not host screaming kids. You can recognize a family-friendly restaurant by the number of other families already there. Restaurants that are baby/toddler-friendly will:

* not mind spilled drinks and strained carrots on the floor
* have plenty of high chairs and booster seats
* provide lids for kids' drinks

* offer menus that are laminated or, better yet, made for coloring
* accommodate special menu requests
* not mind if you breastfeed

Hint: If the owner's first reaction is to pinch your tot's chubby cheeks, then you're probably in the right place.

PREPARE FOR THE EXPERIENCE
TIME

Pick the right time to go. If your baby is a light sleeper, don't go during her nap time. If your baby is a sound sleeper, nap time might be ideal.

GEAR

Make sure your gear is organized and that you're ready with formula, diapers, wipes, a blanket, favorite toys, snacks, and books. Having these comfort items handy will make your time at the restaurant less frantic and will make your tot's experience less overwhelming.

STROLLER ACCESS

Find out ahead of time if the restaurant has room to park a stroller next to your table. Many restaurants will ask you to leave the stroller by the front door. Yet if your tot falls asleep on the way to the restaurant, not having to wake him in order to get settled is priceless.

ENTERTAINMENT

Restaurants with themes or other entertainment are great for buying time between when you order and when the food arrives.

KNOW WHERE YOU'RE GOING

If you're planning on driving, it is worth a quick call to find out if the restaurant has its own lot or if you're going to be street parking. Given all the stuff you're likely to be lugging, you might opt for a restaurant with a parking lot (or one that's within walking distance from home).

Hint: If there is no lot, drop Mom/Dad and Baby off before spending the next half hour looking for a spot.

CHECK THE VOLUME

A noisy restaurant can be very good or very bad—depending on what type of child you have. Most parents prefer louder restaurants because the sound drowns out crying and other drama that is likely to occur. And infants will generally sleep through steady background restaurant noise.

Hint: Places that have big swings in volume owing to cheering crowds or live entertainment are less conducive to sleeping. Consistent "white noise" seems to work best.

PREPARE FOR "CODE BROWN"

According to Murphy's Law, the second you sit down and think you're ready to order, your tot is going to poop. Few things are worse than having to change a diaper on the floor of a dirty bathroom, or trying to coax a half-trained toddler to go potty on a dirty toilet seat.

Hint: Call ahead to find out if the bathroom has a changing station.

BE AWARE AT THE RESTAURANT
LOOK FOR QUICK AND EFFICIENT SERVICE

Nobody likes waiting—especially kids. There are three factors involved in how efficient the service is:

1. *Getting a Table:* Most parents find anything more than a five-minute waiting time to be a deal breaker.
2. *Getting Your Food:* Little people have little attention spans, especially if they're hungry. Ask for snacks like bread, appetizers, and drinks as soon as you sit down (better yet, bring your own).

3. *Getting Your Check:* Getting out the door before the meltdown occurs is in everybody's interest. Ask for the check well before you've finished your meal.

BE FLEXIBLE

Realize that you can't always rationalize your tot into sleeping or eating on demand. Chances are good that you'll spend some time walking your restless toddler around the restaurant or outside while you're waiting for your food. There will be times when you have to pack up and leave early.

If you don't succeed at first, just try again. Knowing how to behave and have fun in a public setting is an important skill for kids to learn.

69

PROTECT BABY FROM THE SUN

NELSON LEE NOVICK

*Dr. Nelson Lee Novick is a clinical professor of dermatology at
the Mount Sinai School of Medicine in New York City, an
attending physician, and a former Outpatient Department clinic
chief in dermatology of the Mount Sinai Medical Center. He also
maintains a private practice in Manhattan. Novick is the author
of nine books, including* Baby Skin: A Leading Dermatologist's
Guide to Infant and Childhood Skin Care.

The sun is not good for your skin and it may be even worse for
your baby's. The overwhelming weight of medical and scientific
evidence points to ultraviolet radiation from the sun (and from
artificial sources, such as tanning parlors) as the cause of 90 percent of precancerous skin growths and skin cancers, including
the potentially lethal form known as malignant melanoma.

An astounding 80 percent of sun damage occurs before age
eighteen. So, as parents, you'll want to do everything in your
power to protect your baby's skin from the health-related and
aesthetic ravages of sun exposure. Fortunately, it is not too hard
to do that.

The best protection and the first rule is to keep your baby out of the sun as much as possible. The sun's rays are most direct and damaging between the hours of 10 A.M. and 2 P.M. from mid-April to mid-October in the northern part of the United States. In the South and West, they may remain intense at these times of day all year round. When possible, plan outings with your infant before or after those times.

If you absolutely must have your baby out at the height of the day, cover him with lightweight clothing: long sleeves, pants, and a broad-brimmed cotton hat. Dark, tightly woven fabrics make the best protection. The tight weave prevents the sun from penetrating and the dark fabric absorbs the rays, making it more effective. Clothing should be loose fitting to allow sweat evaporation. Use a stroller with a hood. Do not rely on shaded locations, such as a beach umbrella, since 60 to 80 percent of the sun's rays can be reflected off sand, water, and concrete.

There has historically been controversy about if and when to use sunscreens on newborns. Physicians questioned whether such young skin was capable of metabolizing the chemicals in sunscreen. To be safe, wait until your baby is at least six months old before using any kind of sunscreen: until then, keep him covered and out of the sun instead.

Look for products that provide at least an SPF 30 rating and contain a combination of zinc oxide and titanium dioxide. These agents provide excellent protection against both UVA and UVB radiation and are not absorbed by the skin. They act as physical agents to literally repel the rays and are referred to as *sunblocks*. Since they sit on the skin and do not bind with it, they are theoretically safer than *sunscreens,* which may contain combinations of salicylates, benzophenones, cinnamates, sulfonic acid derivatives, and para-aminobenzoic acid (PABA) by-products. Sunscreens attach to the skin and work by capturing and neutralizing incoming ultraviolet radiation so these are less safe for Baby. To test a sun protection product on your baby's skin, apply a dime-sized amount once a day to Baby's temple for a week. If a rash does not develop, use the product.

Be aware that products labeled for children are not much different from those made for adults, apart from their colorful packaging and cartoon characters adorning the bottles. No matter which product you choose, it is best to apply it to dry skin before going outdoors and to reapply it every two hours, especially if your child is perspiring or has been in the water. Be sure to apply a sufficient amount to adequately cover all exposed areas, including the ears and the lips, which can be protected with a lip balm containing sunscreen. And don't skimp. The more liberally you apply these products, the better the protection.

Keeping your infant's and children's skin healthy and young looking long after they have grown up all starts in your hands. Begin to protect them from the sun right now, while they are still babies.

70

RECOGNIZE AND HANDLE EAR INFECTIONS

Donald W. Schiff

Dr. Donald W. Schiff is a professor of pediatrics at

the University of Colorado School of Medicine and an

attending physician at the Children's Hospital in Denver. He

is the co-author of Guide to Your Child's Symptoms *by*

the American Academy of Pediatrics.

E ar infections in young children are often a consequence of the common cold. A baby's discomfort—and his inability to communicate what's causing it—can be very stressful for parents. Symptoms like crying, fever, poor appetite, and general misery in babies with a runny nose and mild cough might be the signs of a middle-ear infection, or they can result from the same basic upper-respiratory infection causing the child's cold.

Pediatricians and parents wish that there was an easy stay-at-home method available to determine the difference, but when this question arises only a pediatrician's exam can offer a reliable answer. Many children will touch their ears whenever discomfort exists anywhere in their body, so even when a baby fusses with his ears, we can be fooled unless we look at the ear's interior. The presence or absence of fever is also an inadequate sign of the possibility of an ear infection.

Although an ear infection is not considered an emergency, it is a source of sufficient pain that deserves diagnosis and treatment. Over the past five years, pediatricians have worked hard to hone their diagnostic skills and distinguish what constitutes an active ear infection, which would benefit from treatment with an antibiotic, from those changes in middle-ear anatomy and function which will return to normal without the intervention of an antibiotic. Doctors generally do a careful examination of the eardrum followed by pneumatic otoscopy (a technique which measures eardrum mobility) to determine whether a true ear infection is present, or if the symptoms are the result of a change in hearing caused by fluid in the middle ear (observed in children older than two years) or of discomfort owing to middle-ear pressure. When visual examination and pneumatic otoscopy are insufficient to determine the ear's exact status, some doctors will take additional measurements to determine middle-ear pressure and the presence of fluid.

If the doctor determines that a middle-ear infection is not present, he or she may suggest using acetaminophen and moisturizing the room air to afford the baby some relief. A single examination of the ear drum can be deceptive, since some children will develop an ear infection later in the course of their cold. Thus, if pain, irritability, and fever increase a day or two after an initial negative examination, it is important to return to the pediatrician for an additional look. A child's response to an upper-respiratory infection is dynamic and can change from day to day, or sometimes even hour to hour. Therefore, if a child's symptoms increase in severity, back to the doctor you should go.

Treatment varies when an active middle-ear infection is diagnosed. Some pediatricians are modifying their advice on treatment programs. In the past, every ear infection was immediately treated with an antibiotic. In many cases today, pediatricians will base the decision of whether or not to prescribe an antibiotic on several criteria. Factors leading to the prescription of an antibiotic are (1) the child is under two years of age, (2) Baby has a significant fever, or (3) Baby is clearly in pain. In other situations, the pediatrician may offer you the option of watchful waiting for twenty-four to forty-eight hours to see which direction the illness is taking. If improving, no antibiotic will be given; if worse, an antibiotic would be prescribed.

So why the hesitancy to use an antibiotic? The primary answer is that most children, particularly those who are mildly ill with their ear infection, recover without needing an antibiotic. Additionally, the wide use of antibiotics in our efforts to control disease has resulted in the development of resistance to antibiotics by the bacteria which cause ear infections, pneumonia, urinary-tract infections, and some life-threatening diseases. By using antibiotics only when we know they will be effective and necessary, we will be able to continue relying on them in treating infections.

71

MANAGE TEETHING

BILL SEARS

Dr. Bill Sears is the author of more than thirty books
on child care and a medical and parenting consultant
for BabyTalk *and* Parenting *magazines. Sears is*
an associate clinical professor of pediatrics at the
University of California, Irvine.

The timing of first teeth is as variable as Baby's first steps. Expect the first pearly white around six months, but teething times are inherited. If you check your own baby book, you may find that your baby's teething schedule resembles yours.

Babies are born with a full set of twenty primary teeth, just inside the gums, waiting for their time to sprout. The lower teeth typically appear before the uppers, and girls teethe slightly earlier than boys. Beginning around six months expect four new teeth every four months until, usually by two-and-a-half years, all the baby teeth show. Teeth come through gums at unusual angles. Some come out straight; others first appear crooked but straighten as they twist their way through. Don't fret about spaces. The spacing of baby teeth does not necessarily reflect how the permanent teeth will appear and it's easier to clean between spaced teeth.

Sharp teeth pushing through sensitive gums do hurt and babies will protest. Here are the nuisances to expect and suggestions to comfort the budding teether:

Drooling. Expect the saliva faucet to be on during teething time. In addition, listen for a sputtering voice. Expect these drool nuisances:

* *Drool Rash:* Baby skin and excessive drool don't mix well, especially when the skin is rubbing against a drool-soaked bedsheet. Expect a red, raised, irritated rash around Baby's lips and chin. Place a drool-absorbing cotton diaper under baby's chin or a towel under the sheet below his mouth. Be sure Baby is lying on his back. Gently wipe excess drool off the skin with lukewarm water and pat dry (don't rub). Lubricate with a mild emollient.
* *Drool Diarrhea:* Expect loose stools and a mild diaper rash during peak teething time. This temporary nuisance self-clears as each teething burst subsides. Apply a barrier ointment to Baby's bottom.

Fever and irritability. The inflammation caused by hard teeth pushing through soft tissue may produce a low fever (101 degrees F) and the symptoms of someone in pain. Ask your pediatrician about using medications such as acetaminophen to relieve teething pain.

Biting. The budding teether longs for something or someone to gnaw on. Teeth marks on crib rails and clicking gums on silver spoons are telltale signs of sore gums. Babies may also nibble on your knuckles, arms, fingers, and sometimes the breast that feeds them. Offer a cool and hard alternative. Gum-soothing favorites are:

* Frozen teething rings
* An ice cube rubbed along Baby's gums
* Frozen juice slushy or Popsicle
* Cold spoons
* Frozen bagel or banana
* Frozen washcloth

As always, supervise to prevent choking on any of these.

Night waking. Growing teeth hurt at night so teething babies wake up a lot. A previously steady sleeper may frequently awaken during peak teething times and may have difficulty resettling into the pre-teething sleep schedule. With your pediatrician's okay, offer a dose of acetaminophen before bedtime, or, if Baby is in severe pain, administer a *onetime* double dose.

Here are some general ways to tell the difference between teething and another illness:

* Babies don't act progressively sicker with teething. When in doubt, have your doctor check it out.
* Teething mucus is clear saliva and doesn't run out of the nose. Cold mucus is thick and yellow. A nasal discharge usually means an allergy or an infection, especially if accompanied by eye drainage.
* Teething rarely causes a fever higher than 101 degrees F.
* Teething may be confused with an earache. Ear pulling in babies is an unreliable sign. Babies probably pull at their ears during teething because of pain radiating from the teeth to the ears. Some babies just like playing with their ears. With an ear infection babies

usually feel more pain when lying down and have accompanying signs of a cold.

Finally, expect your baby to need more holding and comforting during teething time. While exhausting for you both, this can be an opportunity for Baby to build trust in you as a source of comfort.

72

CARE FOR BABY'S TEETH

Fred Ferguson

Dr. Fred Ferguson is professor of pediatric dentistry and associate professor in the Department of Pediatric Medicine at University Hospital at SUNY Stony Brook, where he is the director of the Craniofacial Cleft Palate Center and the Dental Care for the Developmentally Disabled Program. He is CEO of About Smiles and Creator of the My Smile Guide website.

As a caregiver, your attention to your baby's mouth is more important than any professional dental care. You can give your child's young healthy smile the best chance to become a mature healthy smile.

TOOTH DECAY

Tooth decay is the *most common contagious chronic child illness*. It is an infection caused by germs that dissolve tooth enamel. Decay happens when Baby's mouth is not cleaned at least several times daily and your child is often fed carbohydrates. This means that milk, fruit juice, any flavored liquid, oral medications, or nutritional supplements (just about anything but water) increase your baby's risk for tooth decay. Sharing cups or utensils or using your saliva to clean around your child's mouth transmits your germs to your child.

You must take responsibility for cleaning your baby's teeth and gums regularly. It is up to you to take care of them. If your baby has a special concern (like a heart deformity or developmental delay), you must be even more attentive to his oral health and seek professional supervision from a pediatric dentist.

DAILY MOUTH CARE

You should know your baby's mouth as well as you know his other end. Follow the routine below several times per day, ideally once before bed and once after each feeding. The last cleaning should be after the last bottle-feeding; before bed is the most important time to remove harmful germs from the teeth and gums, *regardless of age*.

* Sit your baby on your lap, facing toward one side.
* Support his head with your arm and hand.
* Wrap a moist gauze or damp washcloth around the index finger of your other hand.
* Use this hand to open the mouth and support the lower jaw.
* Use your wrapped finger to wipe the roof of your baby's mouth, tongue, cheeks, and gums.
* Once teeth appear, clean them with gauze, a damp washcloth, or a very soft toothbrush made for children.
* At about 6 months of age, start using a pea-sized amount of fluoride toothpaste. If your child does not like the taste, it's okay not to use it. The toothbrushing is what is most important.

DENTAL VISITS

Your baby's first visit should take place around the first year as soon as teeth begin to appear. After that, plan on 1 to 2 visits per year for checkups. You can check for cavities at home by looking near the upper front teeth for white spots at the gum line. And keep in mind that while dental visits are very important, they are not a substitute for caring for your baby's mouth every day.

OTHER TIPS

* Start your baby drinking water as soon as she can grasp a cup and use water for thirst between feedings instead of juice or formula. Save milk formula for feeding times. If your baby needs nutritional supplements for weight gain, do mouth wiping more often.
* If your community does not have fluoride in the water, see your pediatrician to discuss alternatives such as a fluoride vitamin.

We are born with good teeth yet we have lifestyles that lead to decay, bleeding gums, loosening of teeth from bone loss, and breath problems. Stick to the routine above and you'll be making the decision to keep your child's smile in outstanding oral health.

73

HELP BABY LEARN LANGUAGE

ALICE STERLING HONIG

Dr. Alice Sterling Honig is a professor of child development
at Syracuse University. She is a Fellow of the American
Psychological Association and of the Society for Research in
Child Development. She contributes regularly as a columnist for
Scholastic Parent and Child *and* Scholastic Early Education.
She is the author of numerous books, including Talking
with Your Baby.

When babies are born, parents dream of a beautiful, healthy, and happy child, who will learn well and eventually get into a good college. Research reveals that the two main ingredients for successful development are loving, attentive care and rich language exchanges. From day 1, talk to your baby! Smile, coo, and tell your baby how delicious he or she is. As your baby starts to make throaty vowel sounds, respond with delight and encouraging talk. "I love to hear you talking to me!" By a few weeks, some babies carry on a "cooing conversation" of more than a dozen talking turns (back and forth communication even without actual words) with a parent. When your young baby coos and you respond with delight, it encourages your baby to communicate more.

Near six months, babies produce lots of consonants such as *d, p, m,* and *n.* Soon, Baby pairs these with a vowel sound, and you hear "da," "pa," "ma," and "na." When Baby doubles these sounds, they turn into the "words" that doting relatives use in many cultures: *mama, nana* for nurse or grandma, *dada* or *papa* for daddy. "Are you calling Dada to pick you up and play with you? Sure, lovey!" says Dad in a high-pitched "parentese" voice, which enhances brain development. Babies listen to parentese with wriggles and grins!

By about ten months, babies use their pointer finger to share events with you. They vocalize with jargon or babbling: long strings of sounds that are hard to figure out! Baby points to Teddy Bear and babbles while drawing your attention. Label the bear "Teddy" aloud to confirm his babble word. Smile and express your pride as you bring over Teddy. Baby can now babble and share socially with you what's going on, especially if you treat early babbles as meaningful.

First words often appear by one year. All year you have been labeling pieces of clothing (shoes, coat, hat), and foods (juice, apple, cookie, Cheerios, meat). During leisurely bath times, use a cheerful singsong voice to label each body part you are washing—name the objects rather than using a pronoun like "it." This way Baby learns the words for tummy and toes as you soap them. While walking with Baby in a stroller outdoors, point out flowers, doggies on the street, snow on the grass, leaves waving on a tree on a windy day. Label actions as Baby puts blocks "in" a container or pours them "out." Your talking helps Baby learn the names for all the fascinating encounters in the world of the nursery and the neighborhood.

Sing simple nursery chants and songs at nap time. By toddlerhood, your child will even hum favorite melodies with a garbled version of the familiar words. By two years, toddlers put two- and three-word phrases together. These phrases express such concepts as wishes ("Want cookie!"), actions ("Papa fix toy!"), location ("Doggie dere!"), and possession ("My doggie!"). Baby is sharing information with you, so listen creatively: "Dat baw" can mean "That's a ball!" or "I want that ball!" Understanding toddler talk, which often leaves out parts of or whole words, is a real challenge for a doting dad or mom!

Reading daily to your baby is your single most powerful tool for encouraging early learning success. Children love to snuggle on your lap for the experience of sharing a picture book together. Start reading simple story lines only as your toddler shows readiness to understand them. Simplify the text in tune with your toddler's level of understanding. Your caring talk, singing, and reading will give a powerful boost to your baby's early language learning.

74

LAUGH WITH BABY

KAREN DEERWESTER

Karen Deerwester is the owner of Family Time Coaching and
Consulting at Family Time Inc. She is the director of the
Mommy and Me Program at B'nai Torah Congregation in Boca
Raton, Florida, the author of Parenting Quick Tips *CD, and*
she serves as the expert on parenting issues for BlueSuitMom.

Falling in love always includes laughing together, and it's no different as you and your baby get to know each other—from the joys of loud, wet raspberries to the surprises a prankster toddler springs on you.

Each parent and each child bring something original and fresh to the relationship. There are no rules. Mom, Dad, friends, and relatives are a child's guide to the wonders of each new day. Laughter is your child's way of saying, "I love this!"

NEWBORNS
Start slowly, especially when your baby is young. Give her time to find her laughter equilibrium, that heightened, alert pleasure

that isn't too much to handle. Laughing with Baby definitely includes making soulful eye contact with her and using a soft cooing voice. Experiment with what captures your baby's attention—is it singsongy sweetness or a teasing whisper? Toes and tummies are the greatest tickle zones. Tummy kissing and piggy-toe rhymes are reliable favorites, but feel free to explore your baby's body for new spots and even add a few giggle-inspiring props. Try blowing through a straw on your baby's neck and wait for the happy coos. Use a feather to tickle around her face. Don't rush these sensations—go slowly and wait for your baby's satisfied smiles.

OLDER BABIES (SIX TO TWELVE MONTHS)

Once your baby is sitting up, get ready for robust laughter and more active play. Your baby is now ready for some rowdy lap rides, bouncing up and down to nursery rhymes like "Humpty Dumpty"—he may even like going upside down. Your baby now loves playing games and he loves gentle surprises—think variations on peek-a-boo and chasing games; think perching stuffed animals on your head and then letting them fall off; think loud, goofy sneezes (aaaaahhhh-CHOO!). After a few times, your baby will laugh before the game gets going because he now knows that fun is ahead.

TODDLERS

Laughing with toddlers opens up two new worlds for you and your child—that of physical humor and that of humor in words. Sometimes there's nothing better than jumping on the bed (of course, supervision required)! All parents need a few reliable slapstick routines—walking into doors (*Ouch!*), tripping over sidewalks (*Yikes!*), or maybe pillow fights (*Help!*).

Let your own inner actor out. If you sing "Three Little Monkeys Jumping on the Bed," your little comedian will join in, too. Get dramatic: add a new inflection to your voice, add your own twists to songs. Once you find a shtick that works, keep it in your repertoire.

You can always go for the laugh by getting things wrong. Toddlers understand the joke of ducks saying "moo." They love mixing up the world—a shirt makes a very funny hat and you can't brush your hair with a fork. Give your toddler lots of opportunities to shout "no" at a shaken-up crazy world. Should Daddy wear baby shoes today? No! Should Mommy drive from the backseat of the car? No! Should we pour the milk on the plate instead of in the glass? No! No! No!

Become a magician in the eyes of your child. Make things appear and disappear. Pull strange things out of your hat. Start putting together your own personal bag of tricks—crazy voices, silly rhymes, goofy characters, and mesmerizing stories. Don't hold back and don't hold it in. Laughter and parenting are all about letting go.

75

ENGAGE BABY IN PLAY

CLAIRE LERNER

Claire Lerner is the co-author of Bringing Up Baby:

Three Steps to Making Good Decisions in Your Child's

First Years *and director of parent education at ZERO*

TO THREE. A clinical social worker, she is also a

columnist for American Baby *magazine.*

Children develop language, cognitive, motor, social, and emotional skills through play. And the beauty of play is that it can happen anytime, anywhere. Some of the best and most meaningful play unfolds during your daily interactions with your child. *You* are your child's favorite "toy."

While positive interactions between parents and children are critical for a child's healthy development, this doesn't mean that you have to (nor is it advisable to) interact with your baby every waking moment of his day. Young children, even babies, need breaks. (And so do parents!)

What babies need most are parents who take the time to tune in to, respect, and nurture their individual needs. You can help your baby reach his full potential by reading his cues, following his lead, and helping him build on his current skills. During play, the goal is to help your child feel a sense of mastery. This means that when he faces a challenge, you don't solve the problem—like placing the puzzle piece where it belongs—but provide the coaching and support he needs to figure it out himself. This approach gives children a sense of competence and pride that motivates them to take on new challenges.

Below are ways to play with your baby by ages and stages. Because *you* are the true expert on your child, be sure to adapt these ideas based on your baby's temperament and preferences.

BIRTH TO SIX MONTHS

The goal for babies in their first few months is to feel calm, safe, and secure in the world so they can focus on learning and bonding with you.

* Try infant massage. This is a great way to connect with your baby and to make her feel loved. (It may soothe you as well!)
* Offer different objects that your baby can explore by grasping, kicking, shaking, banging, and mouthing. This engages your baby's senses and helps her learn about the properties of objects and how they work.
* Read with your baby. Reading engages your baby's interest in the world and is a wonderful way for the two of you to bond.

SIX TO TWELVE MONTHS

At this stage, babies are learning about cause and effect and how they can make things happen: "If I push this button, I can get the toy to make a sound." "When I pick my arms up, Mom and Dad will pick me up."

* Choose activities that involve cause and effect, such as pop-up toys and busy boxes.
* Respond to your baby's cues. If she is interested in a particular

object, show it to her. When she "tells" you she's getting over-whelmed, take a break from play. This lets your baby know she can make things happen (or stop them from happening!) by using sounds and gestures to communicate.

TWELVE TO EIGHTEEN MONTHS

In their second year, toddlers develop many complex physical, cognitive, and language skills. They become excellent problem solvers and are very skilled at imitating what they see in "real life."

* Introduce activities that pose a challenge for your child to master. For example, toys like shape sorters and nesting cups help children learn how things fit together.
* Offer toys that imitate real life, such as plastic food, farm animals, and kid-sized household tools.
* Engage your toddler's help with everyday routines such as tooth brushing and hair combing. This will teach him important self-help skills and make him feel competent.

EIGHTEEN TO TWENTY-FOUR MONTHS

Toddlers are now moving full speed ahead into the world of imagination and pretend. This is critical for developing symbolic thinking skills, which are necessary for learning to read and understand math and science concepts.

* Encourage your child's creativity. Provide props like dress-up clothes, action and animal figures, blocks, and art supplies. Follow your child's lead in building the stories; this helps her develop her own ideas and thinking skills.
* Read. Let your child explore books in whatever way he likes. The goal is for him to love books, not necessarily to get through every page.

76

CHOOSE TOYS

Kathy A. Hirsh-Pasek and
Roberta Michnick Golinkoff

Kathy A. Hirsh-Pasek and Roberta Michnick Golinkoff
are the authors of Einstein Never Used Flash Cards: How
Our Children Really Learn and Why They Need to
Play More and Memorize Less. *Their book was a winner*
of the Books for a Better Life Award.

Baby aisles used to be reserved for carriages and diapers. Somewhere around the turn of this century, however, there was a proliferation of toys designed to provide babies with a head start in literacy and mathematics. Where did the rattles and cuddly creatures of yesteryear go? In this new era, choosing toys that engage babies can be an expensive and daunting task! Here we offer secrets that won't break the budget, and that come with child psychologists' seal of approval.

KNOW YOUR CUSTOMER
Thanks to science, we now know a ton about infant and toddler capabilities at different ages and stages. Though infants appear

inert, even newborns are dynamic explorers of their world. Newborns analyze speech, are calmed by music, and focus on interesting sights. By six months, babies are reaching and grasping, cooing and babbling, and beginning to move around. One-year-olds add standing to their repertoire, some first words, and myriad social behaviors that, without much language, command any adult to obey those wishes within their imperial realm. We should buy toys that suit the active child, that allow for exploration rather than passive memorization, and that celebrate complexities inherent in the simple things in life. Children's toys can be props that spur activity and inquiry.

TOYS SHOULD BE 90 PERCENT CHILD AND 10 PERCENT TOY

The best toys enlist the child's participation and ignite the imagination. For infants, toys that vary in textures (rough and smooth), produce sounds (bells and rattles), move (in the wind or have moving parts), and are brightly colored top the list. Stuffed animals and mobiles that can be grasped or turned put our babies in the driver's seat. Toys that children watch passively are not ideal—at any age. As children get older, look for toys that allow for multiple uses with multiple pieces. As infants turn into toddlers, they increasingly make objects by drawing or scribbling or constructing with magnet, train, or block sets.

Today's toys often have 10 percent input from a child who does little more than turn on a video or respond to a computerized gadget. Ask yourself, Does the toy I am buying put babies at command central or does the toy make all the decisions?

TOYS CAN BE AU NATUREL

Here is the best news: perfect toys require little or no investment. For newborns, toes and fingers are fabulous toys. They move, feel, and touch. Crumpled paper and pillow mountains offer props for adventurous (and well-supervised!) babies. Babies may enjoy creating rhythms with pots, plastic containers, and spatulas. Forts made from couch pillows encourage hiding and story time. Large boxes become taxi cabs and boats! Old clothes and masks make for great pretending. And nothing beats water painting with a big paint brush on sidewalks or in a yard.

SPEND LESS AND GET MORE

Granted, we don't recommend giving crumpled papers at baby showers and birthday parties. What might you *buy?* Rattles, stuffed animals, mobiles, art supplies, and construction toys are long-standing favorites for good reasons. They help children learn language, math, and science concepts, and, when used with a peer or parent, they also encourage important social skills.

77

INSTILL VALUES
IN YOUR BABY

MICHELE BORBA

Dr. Michele Borba is the author of twenty books, including

12 Simple Secrets Real Moms Know: Getting Back to

Basics and Raising Happy Kids, No More Misbehavin',

and Parents Do Make a Difference.

Suppose it was possible to decide exactly what kind of person your baby would become. Now imagine that you can inspire or nurture these values in your baby and family, a goal that will help you create the best legacy to leave your baby.

You will use this framework to develop a moral compass in your child that will guide his behavior for the rest of his life. It is what will guide your daily actions and help you stick to what matters in your parenting. It will become your central mantra for your day-to-day interactions with your baby. It will help you make decisions based on what you know is right for your child, and reduce guilt, stress, and second-guessing. So let's get started in creating your legacy!

STEP 1: CREATE A LIST OF YOUR VALUES

Wait until your baby is asleep, get focused, and leave enough time to really think. Take out your laptop or pad and pencil. Now answer this question: What traits or values do you hope your baby will possess as an adult? These will be your greatest wish. Write down at least ten traits. To get you started, here are a few that parents typically choose. Pick only ones that are most important to you:

Compassionate	Respectful
Responsible	Persevering
Honest	Trustworthy
Peaceful	Resourceful
Courteous	Fair
Charitable	Joyful
Sensitive	Grateful

STEP 2: CHOOSE YOUR TOP THREE FAMILY VALUES

Now reread your list. Which traits really matter to you the most? Start crossing off those that aren't as important to you until you finally have your top two to five family values. Next, ask yourself why you chose them. Writing your thoughts down will allow you to read them again and again over the years and will help reinforce what matters most in your parenting. Here are a few ways to preserve your ideas:

* Collect inspirational quotes that match your values. Print them on cards and place them where you'll be sure to read them. (e.g., in your organizer or taped to your bathroom mirror).
* Write a letter to yourself stating why you believe so strongly in your vision. On a specific day each year (such as on your birthday, Christmas, or Valentine's Day), reread your message.

* Tell a close friend and then ask her to "gently" remind you every so often of your values.
* Start a parent journal and write your vision boldly on the opening page, highlighting one core value.

STEP 3: USE THE VALUE IN YOUR DAILY LIFE

Finally, you need to make sure you are using this value in your own everyday behavior so that your child can actually see it in action and learn from you. Intentionally start looking for ways to tune up your chosen value and start practicing now. If you think courtesy is important, then intentionally start being more courteous. If self-control is your core value, this is the time to start taking those deep breaths and counting to ten. Remember to reinforce a behavior with your child whenever he or she displays the value. "I loved how you smiled at Grandma. That was really kind. Did you see how her face lit up?" Be sure you name the value, and tell your child exactly how it made a difference.

If you take time to reflect on what kind of parent you want to be and the kind of values you want to instill in your baby, you are more likely to have your wish come true and to create a lasting legacy for your child.

78

MANAGE SEPARATION ANXIETY

Martha Farrell Erickson

Dr. Martha Farrell Erickson is a senior fellow and director of the University of Minnesota's Harris Training Programs in Infant and Toddler Development. She is the author of Infants, Toddlers, and Families: A Framework for Support and Intervention, *and her weekly column, "Growing Concerns," appears in newspapers and magazines around the country. Erickson developed the intervention program STEEP (Steps Toward Effective, Enjoyable Parenting) and was the principal investigator in the Motherhood Study, a groundbreaking analysis of mothers' beliefs and concerns.*

Your ten-month-old baby chuckled as his new babysitter played peek-a-boo with him. Breathing a sigh of relief, you started to sneak out the door for your long-awaited evening out. But before you could close the door behind you, your baby noticed and began to scream.

You will likely recognize this scene and the feelings it evokes—from empathy for your distressed baby, to frustration and resentment over your loss of freedom. But despite the temporary discomfort for both Baby and you, separation anxiety is a perfectly normal and healthy phenomenon that begins at seven to eight months and typically ends at age two and a half.

For the first year of life, parents are the center of a baby's world. Understandably, a baby feels most secure when a loving parent is within arm's reach. When that security is threatened in even the smallest way, Baby emits a loud wail in protest. With time and experience, Baby gradually learns that although parents sometimes leave, they will always return to provide tender, loving care. That knowledge allows the older baby or toddler to tolerate longer separations—or to venture off independently for longer periods of time.

Even at later ages, it's common for a child to experience brief periods of separation anxiety. For example, new steps for the child—such as entering child care, starting school, or going to camp—can trigger feelings of insecurity. Or when a new baby, family conflict, or other major change upsets the family balance, a child may lapse into earlier patterns of separation anxiety. This can manifest itself in crying when a parent leaves even for a very brief time, clinging tightly to a parent in a new situation, or being hesitant to play and explore even with a parent nearby.

Here are some steps you can take to smooth the way for easier separations for your baby and yourself:

* *From the earliest weeks of your baby's life, take time away for yourself.* This allows you to be refreshed and it helps your baby get accustomed to brief separations (two to three hours).

* *Be matter-of-fact when leaving your child.* Even before your baby understands words, get into the habit of saying a warm goodbye, then smiling and waving as you go out the door. If you look ambivalent about leaving, your child will pick up on that and become more upset. And sneaking out will only increase your child's anxiety that you might leave unannounced.

* *If your baby goes to child care, slow down the getting-ready process in the mornings.* The stress of being rushed exacerbates separation anxiety. So get up a few minutes earlier and allow time for a relaxed snuggle or a favorite song or story.

* *Encourage "transition objects."* Babies and young children derive great comfort from blankies, teddy bears, or even a flannel shirt that smells like Mom. Follow your baby's cues in identifying something that helps him feel close to you even when you're away.

* *Relish the reunion.* After a separation, greet both your baby and the caregiver warmly and have them show you what they did while you were away. If your words and behavior say that you view the caregiver as a safe, fun person, your baby will be more likely to see him or her that way too.

* *Be alert to separation difficulties that go beyond what is typical.* For example, if your baby consistently doesn't settle down after you leave, the problem may be that the babysitter or child-care setting is inadequate. Or, if your baby's separation anxiety is intense, prolonged, and occurs in a variety of situations, there may be an underlying problem that requires special attention. In that case, or if significant separation anxiety extends beyond the preschool period, consult your pediatrician.

79

MAINTAIN FRIENDSHIPS WITH CHILDLESS FRIENDS

MARLA PAUL

Marla Paul is the author of The Friendship Crisis:

Finding, Making, and Keeping Friends When You're Not a

Kid Anymore. *She has been a longtime friendship columnist for*

a nationally syndicated section of the Chicago Tribune.

Paul has been a friendship adviser for Ladies' Home Journal

and Cosmopolitan *magazines.*

P regnant women fib to their single friends without even realizing it. When they say, "Our friendship will never change!," they think it's true. They certainly want it to be.

But children change everything. Your marriage will undergo a tectonic shift after a baby is born; why wouldn't your friendships?

You will inevitably become buddies with other mothers of young children with whom you can commiserate about sleep deprivation and the dearth of reliable babysitters, but don't lose sight of your childless pals. Older friends will remind you of who you were before you had a child. That's invaluable because sometimes "you" can get lost in your mom role.

The key to maintaining relationships with your childless friends is for both of you to acknowledge (ahead of time, if possible) that your bonds will be stretched for a while. Tell your pals you will love them as much as before, but your time and attention will be largely usurped—particularly in the beginning—by that squalling—oops, we mean adorable—infant. If you've already had the baby and realize you haven't called your best friend in two months (she always has to call you), thank her and reassure her that you will be back.

While no one can blame you for being madly in love with your infant, your pals will not be nearly as infatuated with or as fascinated by her as you are. So share the latest baby news with a friend, but don't blather endlessly. Remember that your pal has a life, too, and keep the conversation balanced. Ask about her work, love life, and dog. Then listen well. You may not relate personally to her boyfriend blues or job woes, but you can still be interested in her feelings about them. Friends care about what their friends are going through.

Be patient with childless friends who don't grasp that you can't hang out with them all Saturday afternoon at the mall or meet for a drink downtown. Explain why. Certainly you'll need to bring the baby along on many outings with pals. But when she gets a little older, leave her with your spouse or a sitter so you and a friend can have some occasional child-free time.

Your friend may be doing most of the accommodating—wedging into your schedule and driving to your place. If possible, head out to her neighborhood once in a while so she feels like you are making an effort. And to keep your friendship fresh, try something new together like seeing an edgy play, a concert, or an author discussing a book.

If a friend does or says something about the baby that upsets you, don't automatically dump her. First, talk to her about it. She may not understand what she did wrong. Lots of relationships are lost because of misunderstandings that are never aired.

Some friendships will fall away after you have a baby, but you can hold on to many of your childless pals with a commitment to your bond. You'll receive many gifts for your new baby. Consider this a gift you give to yourself.

80

MEET NEW PARENTS

LOLITA CARRICO

Lolita Carrico is the founder of Modern Mom, an organization

dedicated to helping women create and maintain balance in their

lives through an online magazine and nationwide Modern Moms

Clubs, groups providing women with an outlet to meet, mingle,

and network with like-minded moms.

Once you've made it through the postpartum haze—those first four to six weeks where feedings, diapering, and getting to know your baby meld into a blur of sleep deprivation—no doubt you'll be craving interaction with other adults. Preferably, you'll want to meet those going through the same experiences as a new parent—those who understand your panic over the varying contents of your baby's diapers, how excited you are to have washed your hair that morning, and how you need a break from constant "baby talk."

Meeting other like-minded parents can prove to be a challenge. Sure, there are new parents everywhere, but to forge relationships with other moms and dads with whom you will have the desire to maintain long-term friendships—those whom you actually *like*—doesn't happen every day.

So what's a new parent looking for friends and support to do?

The best tip I got as a new mom-to-be was to arrange a reunion of our fellow childbirth class participants. Contact your instructor for a class roster and take the initiative to schedule a gathering with the other participants. The ideal time to reconnect with the group will be when the babies are around four months old—the little ones are just beginning to be interactive and aware of their surroundings, and, more important, you are as far out of "the haze" as you will get for a while. Meet the couples at a park or someplace low key and convenient, have everyone bring snacks, and enjoy the time sharing your birth stories and how you're managing. Another couple from our childbirth class whom we reconnected with at our "reunion" has become our closest friends, and our children (who have known each other since they were four months old and we have the photos to prove it!) have grown to be best buds as well.

Your local "Mommy and Me" classes are also a fabulous resource. (Most are open to dads, too!) Depending on where you live, you likely have various venues offering such classes, including yoga studios, children's gyms, the YMCA, and churches or temples. One of my favorite classes is Stroller Strides—fitness groups that allow you to meet other parents and their babies while getting outdoors for some heart-pumping exercise.

When at playgrounds, make an effort to talk with the other parents—you'll likely find that many of you with babies of a similar age frequent local parks around the same time because of similar nap times and feeding schedules. Set up regular park dates to meet, chat, and play.

Formal parenting groups are typically membership based and offer a variety of local events for a nominal annual fee. These may include playgroups, Mom's Nights Out, family picnics, exercise teams, and more. These groups are typically targeted to stay-at-home parents, working parents, or particular ethnic groups. Most organizations offer websites devoted to their local chapters with event listings and membership information.

For working parents, meeting other new parents is often a bigger challenge, so be proactive and set up weekend or weeknight get-togethers with the other parents from day care. Or, if you have a sizable workplace, post a note in common areas and start a new parents' group that meets regularly for lunch and outside of work with the kids.

Finally, use the Internet. Many websites offer regionally focused boards filled with other parents looking for support groups and activities.

Regardless of how you choose to seek out other new parents, remember to get out there, keep an open mind, and have fun. (Mommy and Me Hip Hop? Why not?) You'll be very likely to find other parents just like you through the process.

81

BUY BABY SHOES

LAURA JANA

Dr. Laura Jana is co-author of Heading Home with Your
Newborn: From Birth to Reality. *She is a practicing
pediatrician in Omaha, Nebraska, where she also owns
and operates an educational child-care center. Jana is the
editor/author of a children's book review column for*
Contemporary Pediatrics, *a member of the LLuminari Expert
Network, and a co-founder of the Doctor Spock Company.*

The purchase of your child's very first baby shoes is a rite of
parenthood. Many of us envision a tiny little bronzed pair
perched upon the mantel years after our children have flown the
coop. Here's how to make sure you purchase the right first pair
for comfort and practicality:

1. KEEP IT SIMPLE. Although you are certainly entitled to make a
   fashion statement out of your baby's feet, remember to factor in both your baby's comfort and your own convenience
   when choosing a pair. You are going to be the one faced with

putting them on and taking them off. Most likely you will develop a newfound appreciation for Velcro!

2. BUY BIG. Assuming your baby isn't walking yet, buying shoes a bit on the roomy side (as long as they are designed to stay on) can make a lot of sense, both fiscally and practically. Not only will they be usable for a bit longer, but they tend to be easier to get on and off.

3. GET A GRIP. While skid-proof soles are not important for babies who have yet to start walking, you will soon find that the smooth, leather-soled "prewalkers" are so called for a reason. Skid-proof soles serve an invaluable purpose once babies reach the age where they are up on their feet and cruising around. If your baby has already arrived at this motor milestone when you set out to purchase your baby's first pair of shoes, remember that what is on the bottom is what counts.

4. THERE ARE NO RIGID REQUIREMENTS. Despite popular opinion and the advice of many a shoe salesman, babies do not require high-top, rigid-soled shoes to support their walking endeavors. Once you determine that your baby's feet are ready for footwear, just remember that it is easiest for babies to learn to walk barefoot because they use their toes to grip the ground below them and balance themselves. A lightweight shoe that allows as much flexibility as possible will serve babies best.

5. THE MORE THE MERRIER. If you're the type of person who gets excited about a great bargain, or simply a parent who doesn't want to get caught short with shoes that no longer fit your baby's feet, consider buying ahead. If you find a pair of really comfortable/cute/convenient and/or economically priced shoes, you

may want to take advantage of the fact that babies (unlike older children) wear just about anything you "tell" them to so long as it is comfortable and buy an extra pair or two in the next size(s) up. While predicting your baby's future shoe size is more difficult when it comes to seasonal shoes like sandals or snow boots, this bulk-purchasing approach works great for foot attire basics such as tennis shoes.

82

START BABY ON SOLID FOODS

LINDA G. HSIEH

Linda G. Hsieh is a registered dietitian and has been a nutrition

educator with Nestlé USA for the past seventeen years.

Starting baby on solid foods is a challenging yet important milestone.

WHEN IS THE RIGHT TIME?

All babies are different. It is most important that your baby be developmentally ready, which usually occurs between four and six months of age. Before this time, most babies are not able to swallow solid foods properly. The instinctive tendency for babies to push food out of their mouths with their tongues (the extrusion reflex) indicates that Baby is not ready to start on solid foods. There is no advantage to feeding your baby solids before four to six months of age, so there is no need to rush.

Here are some key factors to signal that your baby is ready. To confirm your instincts, always ask your health-care provider.

1. Baby is able to sit up with some support. Either she will be requiring support from your arm, or, if sitting up in a chair, she will be leaning on the back or arms of the chair.
2. Baby watches you eat and appears to want to taste what you are eating.
3. Baby likes to put things in her mouth.
4. Baby's extrusion reflex is gone.
5. Baby is able to turn her head away to let you know she does not want anymore.

WHAT FOODS DO I START WITH?

The first solid foods are semiliquids—just a little thicker than breast milk. You can gradually increase the texture as Baby gets older and is able to tolerate it. Allow three days after introducing a new food before starting Baby on another new food to see if your baby has any sensitivities or allergies to the original food.

To introduce new foods to your baby:

1. At 4 to 6 months, start with single grained, iron fortified cereal, like rice cereal. Use a spoon rather than a bottle. Mix cereal with breast milk, formula, or water so that it is only slightly thicker than breast milk; 4–8 tablespoons per day should be adequate in addition to regular breastfeeding or formula feeding.
2. At 6 to 8 months, introduce cooked strained vegetables (yellow vegetables first like butternut squash, sweet potatoes, and carrots, and then the green ones like spinach and broccoli) and strained fruits (apple, peaches, and pears); 3–4 tablespoons per day in addition to regular milk feedings should suffice.
3. At 7 to 9 months, try cooked and mashed vegetables and mashed fruit. Avoid choking hazard foods like cherries and grapes.

Noncitrus fruit juice diluted with one part water can be introduced—limit your baby to no more than 4 ounces of juice per day. Consider trying finger foods like crackers, toast, and dry, ready-to-eat oat cereal.

4. At 9 to 12 months, try cooked and diced vegetables or soft pieces of raw or cooked fruit (7–8 tablespoons per day). Introduce proteins like minced meats or cottage cheese (4–8 tablespoons per day). Try hard-cooked egg yolk. Mixed foods like casseroles (e.g., with pasta and chicken or meat) can be introduced at this age.

There are a few foods and habits to avoid:

1. Honey has been associated with a life-threatening illness in babies under a year old; do not give your child honey before age 1.
2. Do not put cereal in your baby's bottles. Old wives' tales indicate this habit will help babies sleep, but this is not true and the cereal can become a choking hazard this way.
3. Avoid whole milk in the first year. It is too tough on Baby's still maturing digestive system.
4. Avoid chopped hot dogs, whole grapes, and other foods that may get caught in Baby's throat.

HOW DO I START AND WHAT SHOULD I KEEP IN MIND?

1. Find a quiet place for the family to eat together.
2. Start by giving your baby a very small serving of the solid food when he is mildly hungry and before he finishes breast milk or formula—he may be more willing to try new foods when not full from liquids.
3. Be sensitive to your baby's cues; if your baby is holding food in his mouth and not swallowing, do not force him to eat more.
4. Keep portions small.

5. If your baby seems not to like a certain food, try, try again. You usually need to expose a child to the same food 8–10 times before he will accept the new flavor and texture.

Throughout the solid food introduction, more food may end up on you, your baby, and the floor than in Baby's mouth, but your baby will still have plenty to eat—solid foods are intended to be supplements for breast milk or formula in the first year.

Enjoy the new discoveries together!

83

WEAN FROM THE BREAST

Heather Kelly

*Heather Kelly is a board-certified lactation consultant and co-
founder of the Manhattan Lactation Group. She is the featured
lactation consultant on the instructional video "The Real Deal on
Breastfeeding" and is on the board of advisers for AlphaMom TV.*

I t is impossible to talk about how to wean a baby from the
breast without first addressing *when* to wean a baby from the
breast. The American Academy of Pediatrics recommends
breastfeeding for at least a year and the World Health Organization recommends breastfeeding for at least two years. Longer
durations of breastfeeding are not only healthier for the infant,
they also make the process of weaning easier and more gradual
for both Mother and Baby. Additionally, the revolution in
breast-pump technology in the last ten years has made it possible
to continue breastfeeding for longer by pumping and bottle-
feeding breast milk.

But what about the how? Gradual weaning is best. In terms of
breast milk production, the more Baby takes, the more you
make. The reverse of this holds for weaning: the less Baby takes,

the less you make. Dropping one feeding at a time and giving your breasts time in between to adjust to the drop in supply is the best way to proceed.

Make sure that your baby is comfortable taking a bottle (or in the case of an older baby or toddler, a sippy cup). Prepare your child for the transition by substituting 2 bottles of pumped breast milk for 2 breastfeeding sessions each day for 2 days. This is in addition to the normal breastfeeding schedule. After your child gets comfortable with the bottle, begin to drop the pumpings one at a time by replacing the pumped milk with a supplement recommended by your doctor. Begin to drop breastfeeding sessions one at a time and replace them with these non–breast milk bottle feedings. Give your breasts a couple of days of reduced feeds so that they can adjust to the fullness and, eventually, the down regulation of milk production.

If you have been exclusively pumping and bottle-feeding expressed breast milk, it is best to drop a pumping at a time. You may want to only partially drain your breasts at each pumping for the first 2 days of the weaning process.

In the case of sudden cessation of breastfeeding, where circumstances require your infant to be removed from your breast immediately, use a pump to wean yourself over the course of 14 days or so; replace the former breastfeeding sessions with pumping sessions and then slowly decrease the number of pumping sessions. Feed the expressed breast milk to your child, unless there is concern about its safety.

Outdated remedies such as binding of the breasts are unnecessary and do very little to help with a healthy weaning process. Rather, it is important to support but not constrict your breasts during weaning by using a normal bra. If there is any engorgement, you can try ice to relieve the pain and swelling. You can also try drinking sage tea or eating sage leaves in a salad. (Sage has been known to decrease supply.) During the weaning process, keep your eye out for plugged ducts, which are temporary lumps in the breast that can be tender but are harmless, versus mastitis, an infection of the breast that in most cases needs to be treated medically. Symptoms of mastitis include extreme tenderness, redness at the affected area, low-grade fever, and flulike symptoms.

You may experience mixed emotions about weaning and might want to pick a time period when you can be available for some extra quality time with your little one. Whenever you wean you should reward yourself for going through this very important rite of passage. You have given your baby optimal nutrition and bonding, and have given yourself the gift of optimal health as well. Congratulations!

84

FEED BABY NUTRITIOUSLY

JAY GORDON

Dr. Jay Gordon is a professor at UCLA Medical School. He is the author of Good Food Today, Great Kids Tomorrow *and the pediatric consultant for* Fit Pregnancy *magazine. He was named "the most influential doctor in America" by the American Academy of Pediatrics' Committee on Television and the Media.*

Many people put more thought into how they feed their dogs than how they feed themselves and their families. We look hard at the latest science for maintaining our pets' health and youthful vitality, and then, on the way home from the pet supply store, we stop at the fast-food restaurant for cheap greasy burgers, fries, chicken fragments, and worse.

There is a mountain of new information available to parents about the effects of a high-fat diet on children. Yet instead of tapping into that research and advice, we tend to rely on the myths we have carried over from one generation to the next: it's important to eat everything on your plate; dairy products have calcium and protein that's essential for healthy bones and bodies; growing children need more protein. Let's start by assuming that almost everything we "know" about childhood nutrition is wrong and let's focus on the new truths about childhood nutrition.

NEWBORNS

Breast milk is the best way to begin optimal newborn and infant nutrition. Breastfeeding protects your baby from ear infections, diarrhea, and countless other illnesses while decreasing Mom's risk of breast cancer, thyroid cancer, anemia, and other problems. There are virtually no routine medications—including most antibiotics, painkillers, and even antidepressants—that prohibit breastfeeding. Check with your doctor to find out which medications do interfere.

Ideally an infant should be exclusively breastfed for his first six months. There are still parenting books and other sources that recommend the outdated idea of giving rice cereal to four-month-olds. Babies who are given rice cereal get more allergies, tend more to obesity, and can get badly constipated. Breast milk has all the nutrients a baby needs for the first six months of life and probably beyond. Sunlight provides all the vitamin D a baby needs, except in special circumstances, and breast milk has plenty of iron, vitamins, and other nutrients.

At four months of age, babies are reaching and grabbing at anything and this is often misinterpreted as a desire for the food parents are eating. If you put some mud on your plate, a four- or five-month-old will reach for it. Amazingly, he'd eat it, too!

SIX MONTHS

Start solids at six months of age with fruits and vegetables. Avoid citrus, tomatoes, and strawberries until a baby's first birthday. Except for those three, offer your six- to nine-month-old lots of healthy organic fruits and vegetables. Ignore books that tell you that feeding is a tremendously scientific endeavor. Buy a carrot, steam the carrot, mash the carrot in a baby food grinder, let it cool, and either spoon-feed or let your baby get his hands on that carrot and eat it.

Try giving solids for one meal a day and eventually more. As for liquids, water is best. Ideally Baby is still being breastfed. If you want to buy milk, look for soy, almond, or organic milk. Note that on some days even a child of six months to a year might prefer a day of breast milk and nothing else. This is fine. Because of its high sugar content, I don't recommend juice.

Begin grains like rice cereal and oatmeal a month or two after beginning fruits and vegetables. Go slowly with grains—I also recommend adding a tablespoon of prune juice to cereals—but feel free to keep introducing your baby to new healthy fruits and vegetables from six months and beyond.

NINE MONTHS

Starting around nine months, add beans because they're a fantastic source of protein, fiber, vitamins, and minerals. The diet I recommend for babies from nine months—and the diet I recommend for all of us throughout our lives—is fruits, veggies, grains, beans, finely chopped pasta, a little olive oil, any mild seasonings but no salt, and a little tofu. If your family eats meat, fish, eggs, or poultry, you can feed it to your child in small quantities and make sure it is organic.

Sugar adversely affects behavior in all children. Keep in mind that during the first two to three years of life, almost 100 percent of what your child eats is controlled by you. It would be lovely to raise a child who thinks that sweets and treats are raspberries, strawberries, blueberries, and sliced watermelon. Around age three, you can try "selling" this diet to your child: "Eating fresh fruits makes you stronger and faster! People who eat lots of cookies and candy and sugar run slower and can't jump as high." A mild exaggeration . . . but it works!

Once you start your baby on a near-perfect diet during the first year of life, a lifelong path of excellent nutrition becomes more obvious and easy to follow.

MAKE BABY FOOD

CAT CORA

*Cat Cora was anointed the first female Iron Chef
and is the author of* Cat Cora's Kitchen: Favorite Meals
for Family and Friends.

Being a food lover, I couldn't wait until I was chopping, pureeing, and macerating food for my little one's budding palate.

Once babies begin eating solid foods, you can start shaping their eating habits by stimulating their palates and teaching them how to eat a variety of nutritious foods. If you curl your nose up at a food and say, "Ewww, yuck!" chances are your child will feel the same way. Use positive reinforcement about different foods, by saying things like "Yummy," but avoid labeling food as good or bad so that you don't impose notions on your child before she has a chance to taste it.

Baby food you make at home can be a pureed version of what you eat yourself. Begin by buying organic, fresh fruits and vegetables as well as meats and poultry, as your budget allows. Clean foods well and remove anything that might be hard to swallow or digest, such as seeds or skins. Don't add salt or sugar to the foods; babies' systems aren't ready for those ingredients and as they grow into youngsters, it's healthier if you continue to limit their intake.

Steam or boil foods that you want to mash or puree. For added flavor, try braising, roasting, and baking foods before pureeing, mashing, or dicing. And gradually add an array of spices without overdoing it. (Avoid anything really spicy like chili flakes, chili powder, or hot peppers.) You can make enough for several meals and preserve the creations in airtight plastic containers, recycled jars, freezer bags, or ice-cube trays.

Once the food is frozen, make sure to let it thaw in the refrigerator or the double boiler if you need to speed up the thawing process. Remember to label all packages of food with the name of the food and the date it was made, so you can rotate the food appropriately. When heating food, stir well so there are no hot spots that might burn your child's mouth. And test the food's temperature by taking a bite before giving it to your baby. A little trick that I use when my son wants his food *now*, but it is too hot to serve, is to toss in a couple of small ice cubes to cool it down quicker. The little extra water won't hurt the food; just stir it in.

Another tip for tiding over your child's hunger, especially a one- to two-year-old, is to give him a simple savory appetizer such as a few crackers and diced cheese, nuts, unsalted pretzels, or carrot sticks with hummus. As with adults, kids like a few hors d'oeuvres before dinner, and, in moderation, an appetizer will not kill their appetite but rather stimulate it.

There are some safety precautions to take when preparing food for your little one. When you start serving chunkier foods, be aware of stringy fibers, pin bones (e.g., in salmon, trout, and other fish), and chunks that are too large. Use your thumb to measure a quarter inch as the maximum chunk width to prevent choking. As for heating, I always prefer a small pan to a microwave, because with the latter foods can get superhot in odd spots and can be dangerous for the child. And, of course, avoid honey because of the possibility of infant botulism.

Here is a recipe for parents and Baby to enjoy together:

SKEWERED SALMON WITH CUCUMBER YOGURT

8 wooden skewers
1 lime, halved
2 tablespoons olive oil
1 6-ounce fillet of salmon, large diced
1 teaspoon ground ginger
1 clove garlic, minced
1 cup plain yogurt
1 small cucumber, peeled and pureed
Salt and pepper to taste
Pita bread

Soak the wooden skewers in water for 30 minutes to 1 hour. Preheat the oven to 400 degrees F. In a small bowl, squeeze the lime and combine with the olive oil. Marinate the salmon for 10 minutes refrigerated. Skewer the salmon and place on a baking sheet covered with foil; place in the oven. Turn the oven to broil and cook for 3 to 4 minutes. The salmon will cook fast because of preheating and then brown lightly on top. In another small bowl, mix the ginger, garlic, yogurt, and cucumber together.

For your baby, remove a portion of salmon from the skewers and mash. Let cool and spoon onto the yogurt sauce and serve. For parents, season the skewers to taste with salt and pepper and serve a couple of skewers with the yogurt sauce spooned over it. Serve with warm pita bread. (A glass of crisp Sauvignon Blanc is the perfect wine accompaniment.)

One day your child may gobble up everything on the plate, which makes you proud of your culinary prowess; other days he may push it around. I have learned not to take it personally but to investigate a little. While he might not be into a particular food at the moment, it could be that the seasoning is off a bit; you have been stimulating your child's palate after all. So give your child small portions and if he wants more, serve more. This way your hard work won't go down the drain.

86

PLAN A VACATION WITH BABY

PAULINE FROMMER

Pauline Frommer is the creator and editor of the Pauline

Frommer guidebooks. She is the co-author of The New World

of Travel *and a winner of a Lowell Thomas Award from the*

Society of American Travel Writers for her magazine work. She

was the editor in chief of Frommer's website and was at its helm

when it won the Webby—People's Voice Award. She appears

weekly on CNN Headline News to discuss travel trends.

W henever anyone asks my father, travel writer Arthur Frommer, for his tips on traveling with small children, he inevitably replies: "I have only one: don't do it!" Shell-shocked from his years of traveling around Europe with me in tow in the days before disposable diapers, he has the unshakable conviction that traveling with children under the age of six is a tremendous waste of time and money.

I couldn't disagree more.

As the beneficiary of those trips, I know they provided an education no school could match. It's for this reason that I always take my daughters along with me when I can.

Here are my tips, born out of experience, both as the child and the parent.

1. TRAVEL WHERE YOU WANT TO GO, NOT WHERE YOU THINK YOU SHOULD GO. You don't have to plan a kiddie vacation; this is particularly true when your child is under age two. It pains me to see parents spending hundreds of dollars to take infants to theme parks. The well-intentioned couple drags the uncomprehending baby through all of the rides until, overstimulated and confused, she inevitably starts fussing and screaming. Save these trips for age six or seven, when the child will actually enjoy it.

   Instead, pick a destination that interests you—keeping in mind that you will have to find a place for the kids to blow off steam once you get there. During toddlerhood a park or playground is all it takes to keep them happy. You simply intersperse adult activities (museums, restaurants) with playtime and everyone wins.

   Except for the jet lag, I've found that traveling to such baby-friendly societies as Ireland, Brazil, and Italy was, in many ways, easier than vacationing at home. I can't tell you the number of times a friendly foreign waiter offered to hold the baby so that we could eat in peace (something that has *never* happened in the United States), or a local, seeing that we were visitors with a young baby, simply came up to chat and offer advice. Babies help us tap into a universal language, and traveling with our daughters has allowed us to get to know dozens of people all over the world.

2. TRAVEL NOW RATHER THAN LATER. Children under two can fly for free (or at greatly reduced rates). So take Baby to all the distant locales that you might not be able to afford when you also have to spring for his ticket.

3. DON'T BRING YOUR WHOLE HOUSE ALONG WITH YOU. Yes, you need to lug more equipment with you when you're taking baby along, but don't go overboard. Bring enough diapers, formula, toys, and books to get you through the plane trip and the first two or three days, and then assume that you'll simply pick up supplies along the way.

4. CONSIDER RENTING AN APARTMENT OR COTTAGE RATHER THAN DOING A HOTEL STAY. Not only is the cost often less, but you'll have the great benefit of a kitchen should you need to warm up milk, or mash bananas for a jet-lagged toddler at 4 A.M. To find an apartment rental, you can try Interhome, one of the largest rental companies in the world, or contact the local tourist board for their recommendations.

5. CONSIDER SWAPPING HOMES. By exchanging the use of your home for a home in your destination you not only save a heckuva lot of money but you can place yourself in a residential area where there will be playgrounds, other parents to advise you on local services, and, best of all, if you swap with another family, a house filled with kiddie necessities. Go online for swap clubs.

6. MAINTAIN FLEXIBILITY TO HANDLE UNPREDICTABLE BABY BEHAVIOR. If your little one acts up in public, walk him away from the people he may be disturbing and try to distract him. There have been times when my husband and I took turns eating in a restaurant while the other strolled outside with the baby. It's not ideal, but it can help get you through a rough spot. On planes, you have fewer places to escape to so be sure to have a bottle or pacifier handy (sucking helps relieve pressure), bring toys, and, if all else fails, remember that you will never, ever see the people in the rows around you again—unless they are staying in your hotel!

87

PACK FOR TRAVEL WITH BABY

NATALIE PECHACEK

*Natalie Pechacek is the co-founder and CEO of
Babies Travel Lite, a service that delivers baby supplies
to travel destinations prior to a family's arrival.*

Packing for travel with your baby can be overwhelming. You might wish you could bring only the bare minimum, but not having enough clothes, wipes, bottles, or sippy cups can make for a more difficult, less comfortable trip.

Be sure to pack everyday items that you take for granted. You don't want to end up in your hotel room without a bottle brush, dish soap, ziplock bags, or something essential like baby spoons.

There are three things that you should always do whether you are traveling for two days or two weeks.

PLAN FOR YOUR TRIP WELL IN ADVANCE

Visualize how your trip will unfold and try to anticipate your baby's needs. Make sure you have the right clothes in the right size. Think about what gear you might need. Either arrange to have it waiting for you at your destination, or, if you are bringing it, make sure you have specialty bags (bags that carry your car seat, stroller, or other gear you might need to check) so your gear is travel ready.

If you are traveling by air don't overlook airline baggage restrictions. Check with your carrier about the limitations and extra charges that might apply, and pack accordingly.

CREATE A PACKING LIST AND USE IT

List everything you think you will need. Include even the most obvious items so nothing gets left behind in the final rush. Check off each item as you pack.

Here are some basic categories for creating your master packing list:

* Clothes
* Formula and food
* Diapers and changing supplies
* Bath supplies
* Bottles, cups, and feeding supplies
* Medical supplies
* Babyproofing supplies
* Sun-care supplies
* Toys
* Gear: stroller, car seat, Pack 'N Play

PREPARE FOR THE UNEXPECTED

It may be easy for you to adjust; it is not so easy for your baby. Weather forecasts are often wrong and indoor temperatures are unpredictable. Pack a variety of clothing to keep your baby comfortable in case it is hotter or colder than you anticipated. Also, your baby may not be sick when you leave home, but you should be prepared. Pack a thermometer and basic medications, and don't forget a dropper.

In addition to worrying about what you will need when you arrive, you need to make sure you have the necessities while en route in case of unexpected delays and unanticipated baby uh-ohs. At a minimum, always have the following when you board:

* Full bottle or sippy cup
* Diapers (24-hour supply)
* Baby wipes (minimum 40)
* Formula (48-hour supply; don't forget the bottled water if you use powder)
* Extra bottle
* Baby food and snacks (2-day supply; don't forget the spoon)
* Change of clothes (2 complete outfits)
* Medicine (all required medication)
* Blanket
* Sweater or light jacket
* Gallon-sized ziplock bags (minimum 3 bags, for holding soiled items)
* Baby lotion (to hide smells in case of an onboard baby emergency)

If you are interested in lightening your load, there are some alternatives to packing and lugging everything yourself.

* *Shop for your supplies when you arrive.* In advance of your trip check online to make sure you will have access to stores that sell the supplies you need. You also need to confirm that they carry the products and the brands you use.
* *Have your baby supplies delivered to your destination.* Use a website that will enable you to shop online for the things you need and

have them waiting for you at your destination. Alternatively, do this yourself by shopping in advance and shipping your supplies ahead.

* *Rent your baby gear at your destination.* Instead of carrying your Pack 'N Play or doing without a high chair, bouncy seat, or some other lifesaving piece of equipment, rent it from a baby equipment rental company at your destination.

88

FLY WITH BABY

Tracy Gallagher

Tracy Gallagher is host of various interstitials and specials on the Travel Channel, including the family show Are We There Yet? *She has been a member of* Redbook *magazine's panel of experts and a spokesperson for Hilton Garden Inn, and she flies more than 80,000 miles per year.*

We've all been guilty of seeing the baby on the airplane in row 6 and praying that we are in row 26. Now that I am a mother, I get those looks of despair and I have a lot more empathy for other families traveling by air. Here are some ways to make your flight easier—and remain friendly with your co-passengers:

1. Ask about discounted airline tickets for kids. Kids age two and under can generally fly for free on your lap or in an empty seat on your flight. But if it is a long flight, a discounted seat may be preferable to risking a baby in your lap for the entirety.

2. Do your homework—figure out which seat on the plane would work best for you. The bulkhead row has more space.

I have even changed a diaper there because airplane bathrooms are cramped and have no changing stations. Another plus: there is no seat in front of the bulkhead for the kids to kick. The downside: no space under the seats to place your diaper bag and other goodies.

3. Not all airlines let you preboard these days, so plan ahead. If getting off the plane first is a priority to you, request a seat at the front. If you want to ensure there is room for all your carry-on bags and stroller, ask for a seat at the back, since passengers who are seated there board first.

4. If your schedule allows, book your flight for off-peak times. Fly on a Tuesday or Wednesday for fewer crowds and not on the first flight of the day with all the business folks. It is also helpful to book a flight when your child would normally sleep. Avoid booking the last flight of the day to reduce your chances of being delayed by facing a lack of alternatives if your flight is canceled because of weather or mechanical problems.

5. Make sure your car seat is government approved to use on a plane. It should say so somewhere on the seat. Call your airline to see if it offers child restraint systems so that you can just check yours in instead of lugging it through the airport. Some foreign airlines do offer child safety seats.

6. On that same note, one product to look into is a Sit 'n' Stroll stroller. It is a stroller that doubles as a child's flight seat. The wheels and handle fold up into the seat.

Special things to pack:

1. In your carry-on be sure to bring snacks and food and extra clothes in case you are delayed. Many airlines don't serve full meals anymore, so plan ahead.

2. If you are on a long flight, consider bringing bottles with bottle liners. It takes up much less space to pack one bottle, a few nipples, and liners, than packing a bunch of bottles. And make sure you give your baby a bottle or pacifier on takeoff and landing to help with the pressure in his ears.

3. Pack activities for even the youngest of babies. A three-month-old can be soothed by looking at pictures in a book on Mommy's lap.

4. A portable DVD player is a great thing to have—just remember to bring headphones for the older child. And even though the American Society of Pediatricians does not recommend children watch videos before the age of two—c'mon! Desperate times call for desperate measures. A slow-paced video can at least distract a fussy baby from crying.

5. Pack all prescription drugs and common cold medicines in your carry-on bag. It is always good to have these on hand, especially if you are traveling to a foreign country where there are different brands of medicine you may not recognize. Also bring your pediatrician's phone number: it is Murphy's Law—kids will get sick on vacation.

Lastly, with all the constantly changing airport security measures, check the government websites www.tsa.gov or www.faa.gov for other helpful information.

89

INTRODUCE BABY TO SWIMMING

KATHY AND ROB MCKAY

Kathy and Rob McKay are the founders of the Lifestyle Swim School at Florida Atlantic University in Boca Raton, Florida, which is renowned for teaching children aged six months to four years to swim. They are the authors of Learn to Swim: Step-by-Step Water Confidence and Safety Skills for Babies and Young Children.

Introducing your baby to swimming should be as natural as child's play—a joyful, gentle journey approached with laughter, a sense of adventure, and fun! Add a warm, clean, clear pool, lots of toys and games, positive parenting, and a relaxed timeframe and you have the recipe for happy, harmonious learning. Teaching your baby to swim at an early age makes perfect sense. Water is part of our essence. It surrounds us in the womb and it nourishes and cleanses us throughout our lives. The joys and benefits of swimming include family bonding, building self-esteem, and setting the stage for a positive attitude toward learning and exploration, which stimulates child development.

Our four "Pearls of the Pool" will introduce your baby to swimming without pressure or force. These ingredients create a child-centered, child-paced optimal environment for learning.

1. PRIOR TO THE POOL

Use bath time as the perfect precursor to the pool. Bath time should be a playful, relaxing ritual performed with soothing tones and a gentle touch. Pick a time when you are not rushed and can be fully present with your child. Sing, giggle, and stroke your baby while he enjoys the warm water. Over time and with consistent practice, your baby will become accustomed to the slight flow of water with little or no fuss.

2. PATIENT PERCEPTIVE PARENT

When your baby hits six months, you can take your bath-time routine into the pool. Children are most secure with a parent in the water. In a new environment, utilizing that bond of trust established since birth keeps her focused on the adventure rather than on separation from you. Walk around the pool with your baby, laughing, chasing toys, jumping from the side, playing games, and singing songs with hand and feet motions ("The People on the Bus," "If You're Happy and You Know It"). As you do in the bath, pour water over her head (cue baby with a 1, 2, 3 count and then pour) in small doses. Phrase your teaching comments in a positive manner. Say "C'mon, let's go chase that toy and put it in the bucket" rather than "Why aren't you kicking?"

Tune in to the needs and readiness of your child. Before adding a new skill, he should be at ease and comfortable with current skills.

3. PEERS PRESENT

Gather friends for water fun and learning. Create a child-friendly pool classroom by adding colorful water toys—balls, watering cans, colanders, water wheels, bath toys, or foam noodles. Babies benefit from watching and playing with their peers and begin learning socialization skills this way. Your group's energy automatically buoys everyone's spirits.

4. PERSISTENT PRACTICE

Frequency, consistency, and repetition over time are key to progressive, natural learning. Initially, optimal water practice is at least four half-hour sessions per week in warm water.

90

RAISE BABY IN A CITY

Kathy Bishop and Julia Whitehead

Kathy Bishop and Julia Whitehead are the co-authors of The City Parent Handbook: The Complete Guide to the Ups and Downs and Ins and Outs of Raising Young Kids in the City.

R aising a child in the city can be daunting: "How are we all going to cram into this apartment?" "And pay off Swanky City School's tuition bill?" "Is our little urban urchin going to become an eyebrow-ringed club kid by fourth grade?" For sure, bringing up Baby in a high-velocity, high-volume city is never dull. Neither are city children! Take advantage of all the city has to offer your child—diversity, culture, choice—and you'll never consider family life elsewhere. Here's some city parent know-how to get you started.

1. BE PROACTIVE. You'll avoid a gazillion headaches if you anticipate issues endemic to city living *before* they arise. Take schools: maybe your suburban compatriots can sign up for nursery school right before Labor Day, but in a competitive city you may need to start the search up to eighteen months sooner. Always get on top of the big stuff early.

Read local parenting guides and city websites, and talk to other parents—though take what you hear on the park bench with a grain of salt—and get organized.

2. STEP OUT WITH BABY. Half the reason you're raising a family in the city is for the culture, right? But all those art galleries and multicultural neighborhoods won't do your child a whit of good if he's exposed only to your home and the playground. Get out there with him from the get-go and he'll become accustomed to different situations, learn to use manners, and, ultimately, "own" the city just as his parents do. And you can enjoy your town *while* parenting. Restaurants, museums, and culture fests of all kinds are perfectly fine for families. Just remember, urban forays with young kids demand strategic thinking: make frequent but short jaunts, avoid the densest hours, plan for fast exits, and build in distractions.

3. RESPECT THE STROLLER. Urban babies spend more time in their strollers than their cribs, so picking a city-suitable vehicle is worth a little legwork. Look for shock-absorbent wheels (a must in pot-holed parts of town), wheel maneuverability (sideways, not just backward and forward), easy collapsibility (gotta get it on the bus), and detachable fabric (urban tykes take their meals on wheels). And don't neglect stroller safety. Use the restraints (always, no matter how big the child) and never stand at the curb with the stroller in the street. Strollers are too low and too far ahead of the supervising adult to be in a driver's field of vision.

4. WIN THE CLUTTER WAR. Fitting a family's worth of possessions into city housing is no piece of cake, particularly since kids' stuff accumulates faster than dirty diapers. Find your inner drill

sergeant and edit early, often, and before you buy—squelch unnecessary purchases before you make them. The lean/mean approach applies to grown-up stuff, too.

5. PREPARE FOR THE PLAYGROUND. Without a backyard, chances are your city tyke will be spending a considerable amount of time in a playground. City families treat the playground as a home away from home and you will, too, so practicing proper playground etiquette is essential:

* Write your name in black marker on any items you'd like to see come home with you. (Toys have a way of looking alike when baby is cranky and you have to get out of Dodge pronto. This way, you'll spot yours easily and so will others.)
* As much fun as it may be for your eleven-month-old to experiment with "different media," sand does not belong on a slide, so make sure he isn't traveling with it.
* The equipment is for everybody—no monopolizing the baby swing.
* It's a good idea to bring little ones to the playground before school lets out and the big kid brigade takes over.

Speaking of safety, here are a couple of playground hazards you may not find in the general literature: Lead can make its way into playground dirt, especially common at spots near high-car volume or low-income housing. And wooden equipment built prior to 2003 may be leaching arsenic from a highly common wood preservative. Washing your kid's hands frequently—and always after a playground visit—will do wonders to minimize ingestion issues.

91

SET A PLAYDATE

BETH TEITELL

Beth Teitell is a columnist for the Boston Herald *and*

the author of From Here to Maternity: The Education

of a Rookie Mom.

N ow that your baby is sleeping through the night—or even if she isn't—it's time to start dating again. Play-dating, that is.

But don't be fooled by the cutesy name. After a few weeks on the circuit you'll be surprised at how frighteningly similar play-dating is to the real thing.

This isn't the kind of thing a grown woman should admit—a happily married mother of two, for goodness sake—but you know what? Asking out other moms makes me nervous. What if she says yes but is secretly dreading the afternoon? What if she doesn't approve of our toys, or I serve cookies made with butter and her child is lactose intolerant? What if I make a pro–*Dora the Explorer* statement and she's one of those anti-TV moms?

Playdates are supposed to be all about the kids, but in the early days, they're too young to speak, let alone to find another child tedious or disagree with his politics. Which means that it's you and the other mom (or dad) who've got to sit there and make small talk for two hours. I don't know about you, but I can discuss baby-food preferences and strollers for only so long.

Unfortunately, there are no self-help guides for this kind of relationship, no book equivalent to those for the lovelorn like *Katie's Mom's Just Not That Into You*. During five years of double dating with my smaller halves by my side, I've witnessed and committed all kinds of mommy dating don'ts. Here are some guidelines for those entering the Mommy Meat Market.

1. DON'T GET TOO INTIMATE TOO SOON. Don't gossip about other moms, kids, day-care providers—or your spouse—on the first playdate. It's a turnoff. And your playdate will wonder if you'll be talking about *her* to Tyler's mom tomorrow at the playground.

2. BE YOURSELF—TO A POINT. Even if plopping your child in front of a video or allowing treats is your usual MO, go slow on the first date. You don't have to feign being an Earth Mother, but you don't have to go full slacker right away either.

3. DON'T BE A DOORMAT. Don't let the other mom turn the playdates into drop-offs, where you end up entertaining both kids while she runs out and gets a manicure and a facial—unless it's pre-agreed and reciprocal, of course! And by the way, don't you be a cad either. Don't send a babysitter along with your child when your date was planning on seeing *you* (that's the Mommy version of standing someone up, you know), and don't cancel a date at the last minute. It's not fair to leave a mom who's eagerly anticipating adult conversation alone.

4. DON'T DISCIPLINE THE OTHER CHILD. Even if he is a little terror, diplomatically move your child—and any breakables you have

around—out of harm's way. And make sure to schedule the next playdate (if there is one) at the other woman's house.

5. DON'T BE SHY ABOUT SETTING BOUNDARIES. If you don't want to extend your get-together into bath time, say so!

6. THERE'S MORE THAN ONE MOMMY IN THE SEA. That's what a veteran of the mommy dating scene told me when I feared I was going to be dumped after my child tracked Play-Doh through our hostess's newly carpeted living room. "Play-date around," this expert said. "You're less likely to get hurt."

92

MANAGE AGGRESSIVE BEHAVIOR

Debbie Glasser

Dr. Debbie Glasser is a licensed clinical psychologist, past chair

of the National Parenting Education Network, and founder of

NewsForParents.org. She is the author of "Positive Parenting,"

a weekly column in the Miami Herald.

What a difference a year makes. Between your baby's first and second birthdays, an amazing transformation takes place. Once crawling across the kitchen floor, your adventurous baby now runs from room to room. Once babbling, she now asks for juice and mimics her favorite farm animals. And once easily redirected from playing with Mommy's glasses to playing with building blocks, she may be less eager to follow your lead. Your growing baby has developed a definite mind of her own!

No doubt it is exciting that your toddler can explore her own world, pursue her own interests, and begin to assert her own feelings. Now here's the challenging part: She knows what she wants and when she wants it, but her language and cognitive skills are still developing. There are times when she can't effectively make her point, solve problems, or cope with frustration. Even the chattiest two-year-old can be challenged when it comes to expressing a range of complex emotions.

So what do busy, independent—and most likely frustrated, hungry, overtired, and overstimulated—toddlers do when they just can't find the words to express themselves? At times, they may kick or bite.

Here's what you need to know:

* *These behaviors aren't intentional.* Your toddler isn't deliberately trying to hurt others or make a scene. She feels out of control and needs your support.
* *Your child isn't a bully.* These behaviors are common during the early years. With your guidance, your child will soon learn alternate ways to express herself.
* *This period will pass.* Every day your child is learning new skills to communicate, resolve conflicts, and cope with frustration.

Here's what you can do:

* *Stay calm.* Maintain your cool so your little one will feel safe and secure. She'll also learn how to control her behavior by watching you.
* *Set loving limits.* Let your child know you understand her feelings but won't allow her to hurt others. For example, say, "It's okay to be angry, but it's not okay to kick. Kicking hurts." If the behaviors continue, calmly remove her from the situation so she can regain her composure. Toddlers are too young to fully understand why aggressive behaviors are unacceptable, so don't dwell on the whys. Instead, focus on helping your child regroup so she can return to more playful and appropriate activities.
* *Be proactive.* Pay attention to when these behaviors typically occur—like when your child is tired, hungry, or frustrated. If she

bites others when she wants a toy at the playground, supervise her play. Bring enough toys for the sandbox and help the children take turns. If she is more likely to kick at the end of the day when she's overtired or hungry, offer healthy snacks throughout the day and schedule quiet time in the early afternoon for her to unwind.

* *Focus on the positive.* Kicking and biting are hard to overlook! But be sure to pay plenty of attention to positive behaviors. Find opportunities to say, "I like the way you're playing nicely" and "Good job taking turns."

* *Nurture a healthy sense of independence.* Offer age-appropriate choices like "What color shirt do you want to wear?" and "Do you want peas or carrots with dinner?" Daily opportunities to assert independence allow toddlers to feel more secure and in control of their environment, which can help prevent tantrums and reduce aggressive behaviors.

* *Develop a "feelings vocabulary."* Point to characters in books and say, "She's smiling. That means she's happy!" Or "Someone took that dog's bone. How do you think he feels?"

* *Seek support.* If kicking and biting behaviors persist, or if you have other behavioral concerns, talk to your pediatrician.

Recognizing complex feelings and expressing them with appropriate actions are skills that take time to develop. Be patient and supportive. Before you know it, your growing toddler will gain more self-control and a greater ability to cope with frustration and handle challenges. And soon she'll spend more time using her mouth for talking and her legs for running and playing!

93

HANDLE TEMPER TANTRUMS

ROBIN GOLDSTEIN

Dr. Robin Goldstein is a child development specialist and

instructor of human development at Johns Hopkins University.

She is the author of The Parenting Bible.

T emper tantrums are a normal part of development. They typically occur between eighteen months and two and a half years and are characterized by screaming, crying, thrashing, and kicking. Temper tantrums happen when toddlers become frustrated and don't have the verbal ability to express themselves or the cognitive maturity to understand why they can't get what they want at the moment. The good news is that in the scheme of development, this is a short-lived phase, often ending by age three, and one you can get through more easily with some understanding and a few pointers.

STRATEGIES

If you work at preventing temper tantrums and dealing with them constructively when they happen, your preparation will pay off. Try to have reasonable expectations for these ages and keep things simple.

Do try to figure out what causes your child to have a temper tantrum and then fix what you believe to be the source of the tantrum. Ask yourself, Is my child tired? Hungry? Getting enough time with me? Making enough choices? Having to share too often? Being stopped too often from touching and exploring?

Don't reason with a toddler. Your child can't understand adult logic and reasoning, even though your explanations make perfect sense to you. Developmentally, your toddler is too egocentric to think about your needs and desires and to understand that temper tantrums are embarrassing and disturbing to you.

Do distract often. Always carry stuff in your pockets, the glove compartment, and diaper bag, so that you can pull it out at any moment to entertain or redirect your child away from a potential tantrum. As soon as you feel a tantrum coming (at home or while out), react quickly by taking out your keys, cell phone, crackers, cookies, juice, a toy, or even candy. Point out something of interest: "Look at that silly hat." "See that bus going by." Sing a familiar song. Say, "You push the stroller." "Help me turn the TV on."

Don't spank or yell at your toddler during a temper tantrum. Your child may imitate you and hit you or others. Spanking or yelling will make the tantrum escalate. Take a deep, slow breath and tell yourself, "I can get through this." Then calmly either distract or, if appropriate, make attempts to give in: "You can have a few M&M's." "One cookie." Neither are unreasonable adjustments or responses—even before dinner.

Do understand that "giving in" at times will never damage or spoil your young child. Instead, your child will feel a sense of love and care from you. That's how "giving in" is interpreted by a young child.

Don't worry about whether your child will take advantage or remember that you gave in; your child reacts differently to each new moment and experience.

Do pay attention to your child's interests. Allow your toddler to touch, look at, and explore things of interest, even if only for a few minutes. Under your supervision, allow your child to use the computer, take some food out of the refrigerator, pour the dog food into the bowl, water the plants, turn the light switch on, look around the hardware store, touch hanging belts in a shop. Your child will feel a sense of satisfaction and have fewer tantrums.

Don't get discouraged. At times, you may have to leave a store or restaurant with your upset child. Take a brief walk and see if a change of scenery is calming. Otherwise, simply go home, and prepare for a fresh start. Keep reminding yourself that occasional temper tantrums are a normal part of the toddler and early preschool years.

BOTTOM LINE

The way you handle temper tantrums will impact your child's ability to deal with frustration. Learning to deal with tantrums in a patient, reasonable manner that is respectful to your child's development, interests, and temperament is good practice and can pave the way to smoother parenting and a happier, calmer child.

94

DISCIPLINE YOUR BABY

Elizabeth Pantley

Elizabeth Pantley is a parenting educator and the author of

many books for parents, including Gentle Baby Care, Kid

Cooperation, *and* The No-Cry Sleep Solution.

You probably can't imagine that your sweet baby will ever have a tantrum or decorate the walls with her crayons. While every child—including yours—will eventually make her share of mischief, discipline doesn't have a specific starting date.

Every interaction you have with your baby teaches her something and it's the cumulative effect of these lessons that will form the basis for the person that she will become. Your baby's ability to understand discipline naturally changes as she grows and develops. Babies learn best with gentle guidance, demonstration, simple words, and lots of repetition. Over time, your little one will learn the meaning of words, such as "no," "stop," and "off," as well as simple sentences, such as "Be gentle with kitty."

No magic formula exists for perfect day-to-day discipline, but as you develop your own approach to raising your child keep in mind that you are a model for your child's behavior. Babies learn as much from watching you and others as they do from personal experience. Because babies do not have good long-term memories, situations will likely repeat until your child can make proper decisions based on past circumstances.

Your baby is unable to make her own choices, which puts you in a very influential position. The philosophies by which you live are those she will accept as the norm. During babyhood, your child will begin to create her impressions of the world and her place in it. She may not say much while she's young, but make no mistake: she takes in every nuance of your actions. When your baby is honoring you with a world-class tantrum or your toddler is battling bedtime, parenting can be difficult. The ways in which you respond to your baby's actions will affect her future behavior. If you treat her with the consideration to which she is due, she will develop trust in you and reciprocate the respect.

Before correcting your baby's behavior, ask yourself these two questions: Why did she do that? How can I teach?

EXAMPLE 1

If your baby slides paper clips into your DVD player, take a moment to ask yourself why she would do this. When you do, you'll realize that she's watched you slide things into the player, so she's just mimicking your actions. You'll realize that she *isn't* misbehaving but rather engaging her developing curiosity about the world. Keep your lessons simple and focused on the most important points. This may be as simple as an explanation and demonstration. "We put DVDs in here, not paper clips. Want to try?"

EXAMPLE 2

The first time your baby rips a page out of a storybook, throws her food off the high chair, or hits a playmate, she will absorb your reaction and use it to guide her future actions. First, remove the book from her hands, or separate her from the playmate. Then apply the most important step—teach how to properly use a book, or explain how to ask politely for a turn with a toy.

There are endless numbers of things you could teach your baby, but not all of them would be necessary or helpful. Your baby doesn't need to know how your hair dryer works, or even what it's for, but she does need to know that it is hot and that she shouldn't touch it. Over time, and with many such lessons, your baby will begin to apply what she's learning in one area to other areas as well.

No one is born knowing how to be a parent. The more you learn, the more prepared you will be to take each new step along with your child as her personality develops. As she grows, her curiosity about life and her increasing skills can begin to put her in situations that require even more guidance. A parent's best disciplinary tools are diligence, repetition, and gentleness.

PLAN A BIRTHDAY PARTY

LINDA KAYE

Linda Kaye is the founder of Birthdaybakers, Partymakers, a New York City company specializing in children's parties and corporate family events, and the author of Linda Kaye's Bake-A-Cake Partybook.

A successful party is one where all of the children have fun. Elaborate and expensive parties do not necessarily make better parties. The following steps are helpful not only for your child's first and second birthdays but for all birthday celebrations to come.

THE GUEST LIST
Often parties for toddlers include family and friends. You'll want to extend invitations to those who have been involved in your child's life, as toddlers feel more secure when surrounded by people they know.

THEME
Select a theme that will be familiar to your child such as a favorite storybook character, TV show, or stuffed animal. Paper goods are generally available for many of these party themes.

INVITATIONS

The invitation should reflect the party theme and include the following:

* *Party Time and Date:* Be sure the party coincides with the time of day your child is most energetic. Ninety minutes is the perfect amount of party time for toddlers.
* *Party Location:* Toddlers enjoy being in a familiar environment. If hosting a party at home, be sure to babyproof the party area and set up a special place for children to play with toys. If there are toys that the birthday child may have trouble sharing, put them out of sight. Keep pets away from the children's play space.
* *RSVP:* Invitations should be sent out approximately 3 weeks before the party date. Request all RSVPs 1 week before the party date.

PARTY ACTIVITIES

The best activities for babies are music and movement, gym time, and animal-themed activities. Begin the program approximately 15 minutes after the party starts. This helps avoid children becoming restless and allows those arriving a little later to join in.

PARTY REFRESHMENTS

When planning the children's food, Cheerios, pizza, baby yogurt, raisins, and bananas are always great ideas. Avoid peanuts and foods that are easy to choke on such as grapes, popcorn, and hot dogs. Each child will most likely be accompanied by one or two adults. It's nice to have an assortment of easy-to-eat finger foods on a buffet for your adult guests.

The design, decoration, and shape possibilities of a birthday cake are endless! Chocolate and vanilla are tried-and-true favorites. Be sure to avoid cakes with nuts or peanut oil, as some children have severe allergies. It is also fun to make a special small cake for your baby to enjoy. You can use the birthday cake as a centerpiece for the children's table before serving.

PARTY FAVORS

Carefully select favors for toddlers. Read package warning labels closely to determine if they are suitable for babies. Personalized sand pails are great for summer parties. Bath toys, stuffed animals, and wooden puzzles are also wonderful options. One substantial favor is usually a better idea than a lot of little items.

PICTURES

Share special milestones that have taken place throughout the year by creating a collage of pictures highlighting Baby's first haircut, first Halloween, and more. Capture the party by giving disposable cameras to all parents or take digital pictures during the party and display them on your TV or computer while guests are still there. They will love seeing themselves and it's a personalized way to end a party.

PARTY FUN

Welcome guests to your party with style! Secure a piece of red bubble wrap to the floor leading from the entry way to the party room. Party guests will love making a grand entrance on this crackling "red carpet." Select a few of your child's favorite CDs that can be played as background music as guests arrive. Balloons are a colorful way to liven up any room. Be sure to keep them high enough so children cannot reach the ribbons. They are a choking hazard for toddlers.

SAVE FOR COLLEGE

Carrie Schwab Pomerantz

Carrie Schwab Pomerantz is the chief strategist for consumer
education at Charles Schwab & Co., Inc. With her father,
Charles Schwab, she is co-author of It Pays to Talk: How
to Have the Essential Conversations with Your Family
About Money and Investing.

As a new parent, you probably already know about the spiraling cost of a college education. And if this trend continues, by the time your baby born in 2006 is ready for four years of college, he or she will need about $205,000 to attend an in-state public university and about $425,000 to attend a private school.

But before you throw your hands up in horror, read on. As a new parent, one of your most valuable assets is time. By starting now, and setting aside some money every year, you will give yourself the best chance to succeed at saving effectively.

START NOW

When it comes to any investment goal, *time*—and the power of *compound interest*—are your best friends. Assuming you have eighteen years before your baby heads to college, and you earn a hypothetical 6 percent annual return, you'll need to save about $515 per month to reach $200,000. If you wait until your child is five years old to begin saving, you'll need to save $850 per month. And if you put it off until your child is age ten, the number jumps to $1,625. It's not just about how much money you have; it's also about how much *time* you have.

CHOOSE THE RIGHT ACCOUNT

Before you simply stash your cash in a CD or savings account, think about opening up a 529 plan or an education savings account (also known as an ESA or Coverdell), both of which may have significant tax advantages. Following is a brief overview of each plan's unique pros and cons. Many families find the best strategy is to use the plans in combination—perhaps investing in a 529 for the lion's share of college expenses, with an ESA or custodial account adding more flexibility.

* A *529 plan* is a state-sponsored program for college. The account belongs to you, not your child, so if your child applies for financial aid, only 5.6 percent of the value will enter the calculation. In contrast, in the case of a custodial account or other asset held in your child's name, a 35 percent assessment can be held against him. With a 529, there are no restrictions if your child chooses a school in another state or a private school. All potential earnings are tax deferred, and you pay no federal taxes on earnings as long as you use the money to pay for IRS-designated "qualified" educational expenses. In most plans you can choose from a selection of age based or static investment portfolios that are managed by the program's fund manager. *Tip:* Before choosing among 529 programs, check your home state's plan for potential state tax savings.

* While anyone at any income level can open a 529 plan, *ESAs* are limited to families whose joint income is less than $220,000 (or $110,000 if you're single). And whereas you can contribute a great deal of money to a 529 plan (often more than $200,000 per child), ESAs are limited to $2,000 annually (or less if you're at the high end of the income eligibility). Tax advantages are similar to 529 plans, but ESAs can be used for all education expenses including certain elementary or secondary school expenses. For financial aid calculations, ESAs are considered assets of the parents.
* A third choice is a *custodial account,* which you manage on behalf of your child until he or she reaches the age of majority (eighteen, twenty-one, or twenty-five, depending on your state). Custodial accounts offer only minor tax advantages, and may significantly affect financial aid. However, because there are no restrictions on how the money can be spent, provided it is for the benefit of your child, this can be a great way to save for extras such as piano lessons or field trips.

INVEST WISELY

While 529 plans typically manage the investments for you, you are responsible for managing your ESA and custodial accounts yourself. To keep pace with the rising cost of college, it's important to invest for growth. Given that your child won't be entering college for many years, we recommend that you invest a significant part of your college fund in a well-diversified mix of stocks or stock funds. Then, gradually move into more conservative investments as college approaches to avoid exposing your portfolio to short-term swings in the market. I recommend moving into conservative investments two years before you need to access the money for your child's college education. Keep in mind that you won't need all four years' worth of expenses in the first year of college, so liquidating the entire account at one time will most likely not be necessary.

DON'T NEGLECT YOUR RETIREMENT SAVINGS
FOR YOUR CHILD'S COLLEGE EDUCATION

A college education can also be funded through scholarships, grants, and financial aid. However, the only way to ensure a secure future—and make sure you don't become a burden on your children as you age—is to take care of your own retirement.

PASS ON YOUR MONEY VALUES AND SKILLS TO YOUR CHILD

Start giving your child an allowance at the age of five or six. This gives her the opportunity to learn the value of money, begin to make budgetary choices, and save—skills she will need for a lifetime and exactly the same skills you are applying now in saving for college. There is no better gift for your child.

97

BREAK THE PACIFIER AND BOTTLE HABIT

MARK L. BRENNER

Mark L. Brenner is the founder of Parent Fitness Training

and the author of a number of books, including Pacifiers,

Blankets, Bottles, & Thumbs: What Every Parent Should

Know About Starting and Stopping.

Transitional objects are familiar, inanimate items that children use to stave off anxiety during times of stress. These can be pacifiers, blankets, bottles, thumbs, and favorite toys. When children become anxious, they experience feelings of uncertainty and instinctively look to their parents to provide security. If that connection or trust is not available, a child may look to an object to fill that role. The legendary late cartoonist Charles Schulz reminded us of children's need for comfort through his character Linus clinging to his favorite blankie. Every child is different, so here are three options to choose from in each case when weaning.

BOTTLES

Children should stop using bottles and move on to sippy cups between 12 and 15 months.

OPTION 1. JUST DO IT!

As with all changes in life, providing a warning is effective. For the bottle, three days' notice will work. Remind your child several times a day that on the third day all bottles will be replaced by sippy cups. Be prepared for the rants and crying. Remain steadfast, calm, and empathetic while saying, "Remember we talked about changing from bottle to sippy cup? I know you can do this."

OPTION 2. THE GRADUAL PHASE-OUT

This moderate approach can be a trap for frequent battles, so be prepared. It works best over a period of about 2 to 3 weeks.

1. Decrease the number of bottles you offer during the day, replacing them with a cup of warm milk or a snack.
2. Phase out the midday bottle first and then the others.
3. Water down the bottles of milk, but serve undiluted milk in a sippy cup. Gradually decrease the milk-to-water ratio.
4. Try using a funny straw—it makes cups more fun to use.

OPTION 3. SNIPPETY SNIP

When your child is out of sight, snip off the end of all bottle nipples. Then, before she asks for it, show her how dangerous the rubber has become. Express genuine concern and surprise. "Look at the rubber tip. That's called jagged. Can you say *jagged?*" Explain that this is dangerous and it makes the rubber taste funny. Make a game of having your child throw the bottles in the trash and to be safe, follow up to make sure they're properly disposed of. If she demands a new bottle, use a calm and reassuring tone to tell her that it is now time for her to pick out a cup to buy. If she insists on wanting a bottle, acknowledge her feelings, but remain firm. This will take many rounds. Be direct, emphatic, and steadfast.

PACIFIERS

Eighteen months is a good point to begin to break the pacifier habit.

OPTION 1. JUST DO IT!

As with the bottles, providing an advance alert allows your child to switch mindsets. Three days' notice will work. Talk about it with your child and on the third day remove all of the pacifiers. Calmly respond to his protests with phrases like "Now you can calm yourself down and that feels good, too!" After 3 days without the pacifier your child will learn the power of self-soothing and self-control. It also helps to support his need to replace the pacifier with a blanket, toy, or stuffed animal.

OPTION 2. PLAY "PILLOW WISH"

Say to your child, "Sometimes wishes come true and sometimes they don't. Tonight we'll play pillow wish." Have your child place all of his pacifiers under his pillow that night. Replace the pacifiers with a new toy he has been wanting so that when he wakes up, he finds the surprise under his pillow. When your child asks for the pacifiers back during moments of frustration, acknowledge his feelings, but remind him of the game: "You miss your pacifier even though you are happy with your wish. Sometimes that happens." (This works with bottles, too.)

OPTION 3. THE LIMIT RULE

Work to modify your child's behavior by limiting pacifier use. Begin by not allowing use anywhere but at home and then limit it to certain rooms within the home. Keep decreasing the rooms in which you allow him to use the pacifier until there are none remaining. Alternatively, you can try a time limitation—like 5 minutes in certain rooms—or limit usage to nap time and bedtime, and eventually only at bedtime until you phase it out completely.

98

TOILET TRAIN

Nathan H. Azrin

Dr. Nathan H. Azrin is a psychologist and professor at
Nova Southeastern University in Fort Lauderdale, Florida.
He is the co-author with R. Foxx of the long-standing popular
book Toilet Training in Less Than a Day, *used by millions of*
parents since its initial publication in 1974.

Though many parents hope that their children will spontaneously learn to urinate in the toilet, toilet training is a social skill that you can't expect to occur without teaching any more than brushing one's teeth or learning to read.

TIMING

At eighteen to twenty-four months of age bladder control is usually sufficient for training to take place. Your child must also be able to walk so that he can quickly get to the potty location. Beyond age and mobility, a decrease in diaper wettings is another indicator of sufficient bladder control, suggesting that he can now hold on to a larger volume of urine. And your child should be able to follow parental directions, a requirement necessary for teaching any social skill.

READINESS TRAINING

Before starting training, it is helpful for your child to observe you or another family member in the act of toileting and for you to narrate the act for him while he is watching.

INTENSIVE TRAINING

The following toilet-training program requires an average of only 4 hours in a single day, rather than the common duration of several months. The toilet training should be framed as a game in which your child will be teaching a doll how to use a toilet. Begin by giving your child as much liquid to drink as possible, using favorites such as soda, juice, and flavored milk. For easy access to drinks, the kitchen is usually the best training location. The high volume of liquids should create urgency for your child to urinate frequently in a short period of time, thereby contributing to the rapid results of training. This continuous drinking should be encouraged during the entire 4-hour period.

STEP 1: LEARNING BY TEACHING

During the first half hour, your child will teach a doll to use the toilet. The doll should be the same gender as your child, should wear pants, and be hollow with two openings, one at the mouth, and one at the seat. Prompt your child to pretend that the doll needs to toilet, then to walk the doll to the potty, lower its undergarments, sit the doll quietly on the potty, and then to offer praise to the doll and a reward for urinating in the potty. Praise your child for the doll's success and offer a liquid reward for the final step.

STEP 2: TOILET APPROACH TRIALS

After the first half hour, direct your child to go to the potty every 15 minutes. Have him lower his pants and sit on the potty for a minimum of 10 minutes or until he urinates. The large volume of liquids he has been drinking should ensure success. Exuberantly praise your child for each urination in the toilet, when he dresses himself, empties the potty bowl in the toilet, flushes, washes his hands, and leaves the bathroom. Use gestures and gentle manual guidance to accompany all of your verbal instructions to ensure that he understands and follows each step. Give him a drink for each successful urination.

Each of the above actions should be accompanied by praise offered with a pleasant voice, an encouraging facial expression, and a kiss or hug. Stay near him throughout each step so that any hesitation in following your instructions is followed within one second by your gentle touch and helpful guidance. Your child should feel continuously praised, embraced, instructed, and guided while playing a fun-filled game.

STEP 3: INDEPENDENCE TRAINING

Gradually reduce the extent of the instructions over the four-hour period as your child learns to follow them. Begin with full explanations, reduce these to one or two words, then to gestures only, then to facial expressions, and finally to no instructions at all, allowing your child to approach the potty and perform all of the actions independently.

DRYNESS TRAINING

Once your child has urinated in the toilet without instructions at least three times, discontinue rewards for urinations; instead, give rewards for being dry. Begin dry rewards immediately. For every fifteen minutes he is dry, give a reward. This will emphasize being dry as the goal, with toilet use as only a means to that end.

ACCIDENTS

When your child wets his pants, do not criticize or scold him. Instead, require that he change himself and do several "pretend trials" in which he pretends to have an urge to urinate, goes quickly to the potty, sits there for a few seconds, and initiates another "pretend" trial.

These guidelines will make toilet training an enjoyable bonding experience for both of you. With a half day and a positive attitude, you should achieve toilet training success.

99

CREATE FAMILY TRADITIONS

Susan Newman

Dr. Susan Newman is a social psychologist and author

of thirteen parenting and relationship books, including

Little Things Long Remembered: Making Your

Children Feel Special Every Day.

W hen we think of traditions, we tend to think of holidays and repeated rituals we learned and loved as children. Holidays are only one small gold mine in the rich landscape of possibilities. Quite unexpectedly, you will create new traditions unique to your growing family.

Contrary to popular belief, the best traditions evolve without effort or precise plan and are self-sustaining. A parent's role is merely to set the stage, offer opportunities, and follow your children's lead. When a suggestion catches a child's fancy or imagination, the tradition falls into place seamlessly. When my son was six years old he asked to stir the pumpkin-pie filling I was preparing for Thanksgiving. Now in his twenties, he makes pumpkin pie every Thanksgiving. Family and friends anticipate it; his early attempts—the pies that looked more like squashed craters with lava oozing over the edges—are a funny part of family lore.

You may request a child's mini–piano concert on a special occasion, and next time that child will beg to play. The family comes to expect the tradition even if only one family member carries it out: Mom's toast, Dad's running of the family meeting complete with toy gavel, Aunt's witty birthday poems.

The most meaningful traditions are often spontaneous, springing from everyday routines: the special "designer" kiss (a peck on the nose, for example) you gave your infant becomes mandatory before bedtime; dancing in the kitchen after dinner; singing in the car on the way to sports practices; the private wink, thumbs-up, or fight cheer as you send your child off to day care or school. These little rituals bring family closer; everyone stores the gesture in his or her memory bank.

The secret ingredient is repetition: blueberry pancakes on Sunday mornings, a jigsaw puzzle left up in a corner to work on whenever there are a few spare minutes, a board game the whole family plays once a month, the fun heightened by traditional ice-cream sundaes or a mammoth bowl of popcorn.

No matter what you try, be sure it's something you want or like to do. Children are very aware of the parent who fakes enjoyment. If you are not having a good time, you take the joy out of it for your children, too.

Traditions shouldn't be work and won't be if everyone's enthusiastic. In our family, on the last night of every vacation the adults prepare an awards ceremony. The sillier the categories and awards the better: for the best sand castle, a plastic shovel; most willing to join in, a box of crayons . . . You get the idea.

If you're adept at making up stories, at bedtime build them around your child's friends and activities; if reading storybooks, sprinkle your child's name into the text whenever possible. Talk about the best and worst part of your child's day; give your talk a name such as Chit-chats, and you may well be Chit-chatting into your child's teen years and beyond.

The uncomplicated things you do together may be so well received that your children request them, and without planning, they become cherished memories of growing up—and of you. You never know what little thing will catch on and strengthen connections—a special chair piled high with pillows for the birthday person, double dessert night announced out of the blue, or your preschooler's catchy jingle that the family ends up still singing when he's college age or older.

When you pay close attention to what delights your children you wind up with a treasure-trove of rituals—the glue that keeps family thriving and happy and your children feeling loved and secure.

100

PLAN YOUR NEXT PREGNANCY

Toni Weschler

*Toni Weschler is a women's health educator and the author of
the best seller* Taking Charge of Your Fertility. *She is also the
co-producer of the book's accompanying software.*

So your first baby was a surprise? Or maybe it took you years
of stress and frustration to finally achieve your dream. Either
way, wouldn't it be nice to have a sense of control over the most
profound decision you will ever make—that of choosing to conceive another child?

Deciding when to have another child is crucial for your mental sanity as well as your physical readiness. The issue of your
mental health is a subjective matter best left to you and your
partner. Fortunately, your physical preparedness is more objec-
tive. Studies show that a healthy time to conceive after the birth
of your last child is eighteen to twenty-four months.

Once you have decided if or when to conceive, you'll need to
dispense with one of the most insidious fertility myths around—
that of the ol' day 14 ovulation. Yes, ovulation may occur on day
14. But it may also occur days before or even weeks after if your

cycle is less regular. And given that your ultimate goal should be to time intercourse around the release of a tiny egg smaller than the period at the end of this sentence, you'll want to learn how to identify when that time will be.

The first part of your cycle, from day 1 of bleeding to ovulation, can vary considerably. The second part of your cycle, from ovulation to the last day before the new period begins, usually has a finite span of twelve to sixteen days. The egg remains alive for a maximum of twenty-four hours, during which it either gets fertilized or disintegrates. In order for conception to occur, *three* factors must be present: the egg, the sperm, and fertile quality cervical fluid which allows sperm to swim through the cervix to reach its destiny with its hot date.

FERTILITY AWARENESS

By observing and charting two primary fertility signs, you can determine whether or not you are fertile each day.

WAKING TEMPERATURE

Taking your oral waking temperature can tell you whether you are ovulating or if you may have a hormonal problem. A normal ovulatory cycle should show two conspicuous phases of temperatures. Your temperatures should fluctuate between a low range before ovulation and a higher range after ovulation, indicating that ovulation has *already* occurred. Before ovulation, waking temperatures will range from 97.0 degrees F to 97.5 degrees F, and after ovulation they will rise to 97.6 degrees F to 98.6 degrees F. They will usually remain elevated until your next period, about two weeks later. But if you were to become pregnant, they would remain high for over eighteen days after ovulation.

To record the most accurate temperatures, you will need to use either a basal or a digital thermometer that shows temperatures in increments of one-tenth rather than two-tenths.

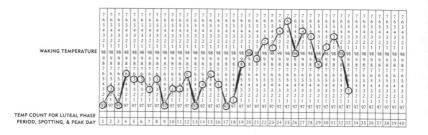

CERVICAL FLUID

After your period, your cervical fluid typically starts to develop in a pattern that becomes wetter as you approach ovulation. After your bleeding ends, you may notice nothing, followed by cervical fluid that often evolves from sticky to creamy and finally to clear, slippery, and stretchy. The most important feature of this extremely fertile cervical fluid is the lubricative quality.

A trick to help you identify the quality of the cervical fluid is to notice what it feels like to run tissue (or your finger) across your vaginal lips. When you are dry, the tissue won't pass across your vaginal lips smoothly. As you approach ovulation, your cervical fluid gets progressively more lubricative, and thus the tissue should glide easily.

USING THE FERTILITY AWARENESS METHOD
FOR PREGNANCY ACHIEVEMENT

1. Take your temperature first thing upon waking each morning to determine if you are ovulating that cycle. If you don't see an obvi-

ous biphasic pattern over the course of the month, you should seek a consultation to make sure that you are indeed ovulating.

2. Time intercourse to occur on all days of wet, slippery cervical fluid. The most fertile day of your cycle will be the last day that you have this slippery-quality cervical fluid, usually occurring before your temperature shift.

3. If your temperature remains high for at least 18 consecutive days, run out to buy that pregnancy test! Congratulations—you have undoubtedly conceived!

EXPERTS' WEBSITES

Sanders, Darcie	204	Adjust to life as a stay-at-home parent	www.spencerandwaters.com
Sarvady, Andrea	78	Swaddle	www.andreasarvady.com
Schatsky, Gary	21	Write a will	www.objectiveadvice.com
Schiff, Donald W.	227	Recognize and handle ear infections	www.expertsmedia.com
Schwab Pomerantz, Carrie	310	Save for college	www.schwab.com
Sears, Bill	230	Manage teething	www.askdrsears.com
Shelov, Steven P.	97	Prevent and treat diaper rash	www.expertsmedia.com
Spade, Kate	94	Pack a diaper bag	www.katespade.com
Spencer, Paula	126	Handle unsolicited parenting advice	www.paulaspencer.com
Steinberg, Laurence	120	Develop good parenting habits	http://astro.temple.edu/~lds
Stern, Loraine	49	Bottle-feed	www.valpeds.com
Straub, Susan	170	Read to baby	www.readtomeprogram.org
Sykes, Lucy	147	Dress your baby	www.lucysykesnewyork.com
Teitell, Beth	295	Set a playdate	www.teitell.com
Thompson, Trisha	99	Practice good diapering etiquette	www.wondertime.com
Tierno, Philip M. Jr.	56	Protect baby from harmful germs	http://microbiology.med.nyu.edu/microbiology/faculty/tierno
Wattenberg, Laura	4	Choose a name	www.babynamewizard.com
Weissbluth, Marc	183	Get baby to sleep through the night	www.sweetbabies.com
Weschler, Toni	324	Plan your next pregnancy	www.tcoyf.com
Weston, Liz Pulliam	7	Budget for a new baby	www.asklizweston.com
Whitehead, Julia	292	Raise baby in a city	www.expertsmedia.com
Widome, Mark	68	Prepare for an emergency	www.expertsmedia.com

CREDITS

"Achieve Balance as a New Parent" © 2006 by Mimi Doe • "Adjust to Life as a Stay-at-Home Parent" © 2006 by Darcie Sanders and Martha M. Bullen • "Babyproof" © 2006 by Debra Smiley Holtzman • "Bathe Your Baby" © 2006 by Lillian McLean Beard, MD • "Be a Great Father" © 2006 by Armin Brott • "Be a Loving Grandparent" © 2006 by Arthur Kornhaber, MD • "Be a Stylish New Mom" © 2006 by Liz Lange Maternity • "Bottle-feed" © 2006 by Loraine Stern, MD • "Break the Pacifier and Bottle Habit" © 2006 by Mark L. Brenner, MFT • "Breastfeed" © 2006 by The Pump Station • "Budget for a New Baby" © 2006 by No More Red Inc. • "Buy Baby Shoes" © 2006 by Laura A. Jana • "Buy Life Insurance" © 2006 by Ben G. Baldwin • "Calm a Crying Baby" © 2006 by Harvey Karp, MD • "Care for a Toddler and a Newborn" © 2006 by Molly Gold • "Care for Baby's Penis" © 2006 by Cara Familian Natterson, MD • "Care for Baby's Teeth" © 2006 by Dr. Fred S. Ferguson • "Choose a Child-Care Option" © 2006 by Ann Douglas • "Choose a Name" © 2006 by Laura Wattenberg • "Choose a Pediatrician" © 2006 by Dr. Michel Cohen • "Choose Between Working and Staying Home" © 2006 by Wendy Sachs • "Choose Toys" © 2006 by Dr. Kathy Hirsh-Pasek and Dr. Roberta M. Golinkoff • "Create Family Traditions" © 2006 by Susan Newman, PhD • "Design a Nursery" © 2006 by Wendy Bellissimo Media, Inc • "Develop Good Parenting Habits" © 2006 by Dr. Laurence Steinberg • "Discipline Your Baby" © 2006 by Elizabeth Pantley • "Distinguish Healthy Versus Sick Signs" © 2006 by Dr. Tanya Remer Altmann • "Do Yoga with Baby" © 2006 by Helen Garabedian • "Document Baby's Life" © 2006 by Lisa Bearnson • "Dress Your Baby" © 2006 by Euan Rellie, Lucy Sykes Rellie, and Lucy Sykes Baby LLC • "Embrace Your Role as a New Mother" © 2006 by Ann Pleshette Murphy, Inc. • "Engage Baby in Play" © 2006 by ZERO TO THREE: National Center for Infants, Toddlers and Families • "Feed Baby Nutritiously" © 2006 by Jay Gordon, MD • "Find Your Inner Patience" © 2006 by Jan Faull • "Fly with Baby" © 2006 by Tracy Gallagher • "Get in Shape After Childbirth" © 2006 by Pamela M. Peeke, MD, MPH, FACP • "Get Baby to Sleep Through the Night" ©

333

• "Read to Baby" © 2006 by Susan Straub • "Recognize and Handle Ear Infections" © 2006 by Donald Schiff, MD • "Recognize Postpartum Depression" © 2006 by The Postpartum Stress Center • "Recover from a C-section" © 2006 by Rita Rubin • "Reduce and Eliminate Stretch Marks" © 2006 by Howard Murad, MD • "Reduce the Risk of SIDs" © 2006 by Fern R. Hauck, MD, MS • "Return to Work" © 2006 by Maria Bailey • "Save for College" © 2006 by Charles Schwab & Co., Inc. • "Select and Install a Car Seat" © 2006 by Jennifer Huebner • "Set a Playdate" © 2006 by Beth Teitell • "Start Baby on Solid Foods" © 2006 by Linda G. Hsieh, RD • "Swaddle" © 2006 by Andrea Sarvady • "Take Care of Yourself as a New Mother" © 2006 by Debra Gilbert Rosenberg • "Take Baby to a Restaurant" © 2006 by OAM Solutions, Inc. • "Teach Baby to Nap" © 2006 by Jodi A. Mindell, PhD • "Teach Baby to Self-Soothe" © 2006 by Suzy Giordano and Lisa Abidin • "Teach Baby to Sign" © 2006 by Baby Signs Inc. • "Toilet Train" © 2006 by Nathan H. Azrin, PhD • "Track Developmental Milestones" © 2006 by Alan Greene, MD, FAAP • "Trust Your Instincts as a New Parent" © 2006 by Lu Hanessian • "Wean from the Breast" © 2006 by Heather Kelly, MA, IBCLC • "Wear Your Baby" © 2006 by Maria Blois • "Work with Baby's Temperament" © 2006 by Jan Kristal • "Write a Will" © 2006 by Gary H. Schatsky

INDEX